CODEX OBSCURA: SECRETS OF THE VOYNICH MANUSCRIPT

by

Domingo Delgado

Frontispiece. The original vellum cover of Beinecke MS 408 (Voynich Manuscript), preserved at Yale University.

Copyright

CODEX OBSCURA: SECRETS OF THE VOYNICH
MANUSCRIPT

TABLE OF CONTENTS

PREFACE: WHY THIS BOOK, WHY NOW?

Figure 1. Johannes Marcus Marci (1595–1667), rector of Charles University and sender of the famous 1665 letter about the manuscript. Context: Marci's 1665 letter links the manuscript to Emperor Rudolf II and set the modern trail of provenance. In plain terms, this is one of the key people whose letter tells us the Voynich was famous—and puzzling—even in the 1600s.

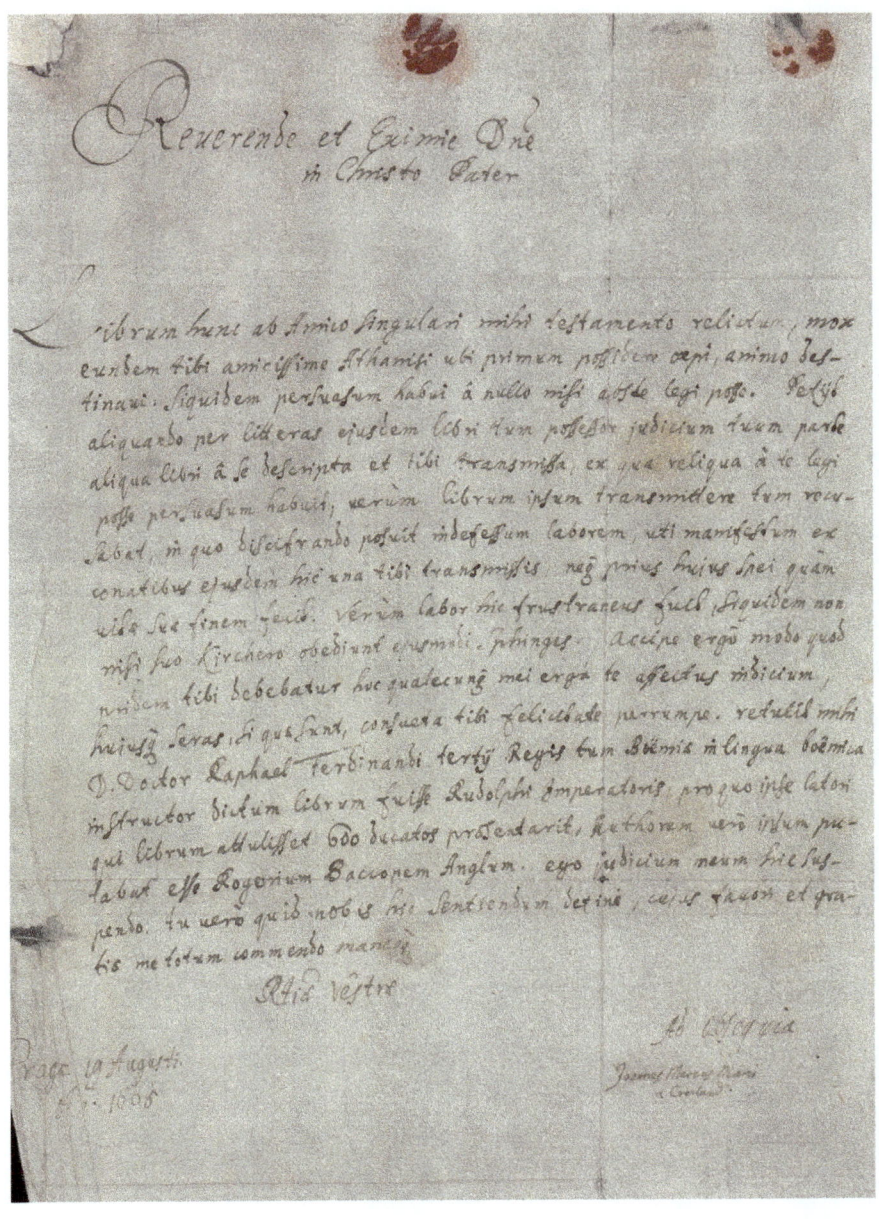

Figure 2. Marci's 1665 letter to Athanasius Kircher mentioning Emperor Rudolf II's ownership. Context: Marci's 1665 letter links the manuscript to Emperor Rudolf II and sets the modern trail of provenance.

Figure 3. Emperor Rudolf II, whose Prague court reportedly owned the Voynich Manuscript. Context: Rudolf II collected alchemical and scientific curiosities at Prague; the Voynich fit his taste perfectly. In plain terms, an emperor bought this mysterious book because he loved strange knowledge.

Figure 4. Michał Wojnicz (Wilfrid Voynich), the bookseller who rediscovered the codex in 1912. Context: Wilfrid Voynich rediscovered the manuscript in 1912 and brought it to modern attention. In plain terms, the book is named after the dealer who found it in a Jesuit library.

Figure 5. Villa Mondragone near Rome, where Voynich acquired the manuscript from Jesuit archives. Context: This Jesuit college is where Wilfrid Voynich rediscovered the manuscript in 1912, purchasing it from their archives. In plain terms, the book was found here, in a library near Rome.

P. ATHANASIVS KIRCHERVS FVLDENSIS
ê *Societ:* Iefu Anno ætatis LIII.

Honoris et observantiæ ergò sculpsit et D.D.C.Bloemaert Romæ 2 Maij A.1655.

Figure 6. Athanasius Kircher, Jesuit polymath and the manuscript's would-be decipherer. Context: Marci sent the codex to Kircher to decode; the letter explicitly mentions Rudolf II's ownership. In plain terms, this was the seventeenth-century "please decrypt this" note that preserved the manuscript's story.

Figure 7. (folio 90r) Typical Voynich herbal folio, the manuscript's largest section. Context: The herbal section comprises the bulk of the manuscript, with hundreds of illustrations of unknown or fantastical plants. In plain terms, most of the book is filled with drawings of mysterious plants like this one.

Figure 8. (folio 68r) Voynich astronomical folio with suns, moons, and stars. Context: The astronomical and astrological folios contain complex diagrams of celestial bodies, often arranged in circular patterns. In plain terms, the book also has many pages with strange drawings of the sun, moon, and stars.

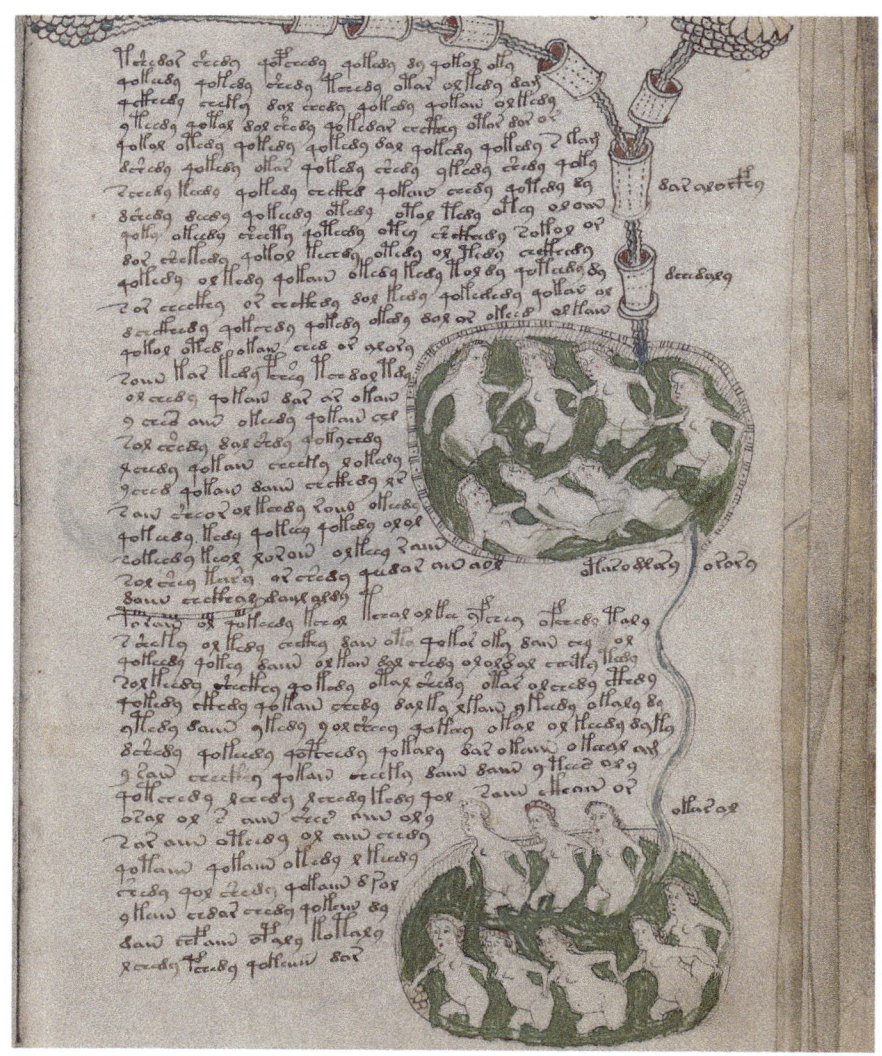

Figure 9. Voynich Manuscript (MS 408), f. 78r. Voynich "balneological" folio depicting bathing women in plumbing-like basins. Context: The so-called "balneological" section features distinctive scenes of nude women in an elaborate, interconnected basins and tubes. In plain terms, this is from a section showing women bathing in bizarre, plumbing-like structures.

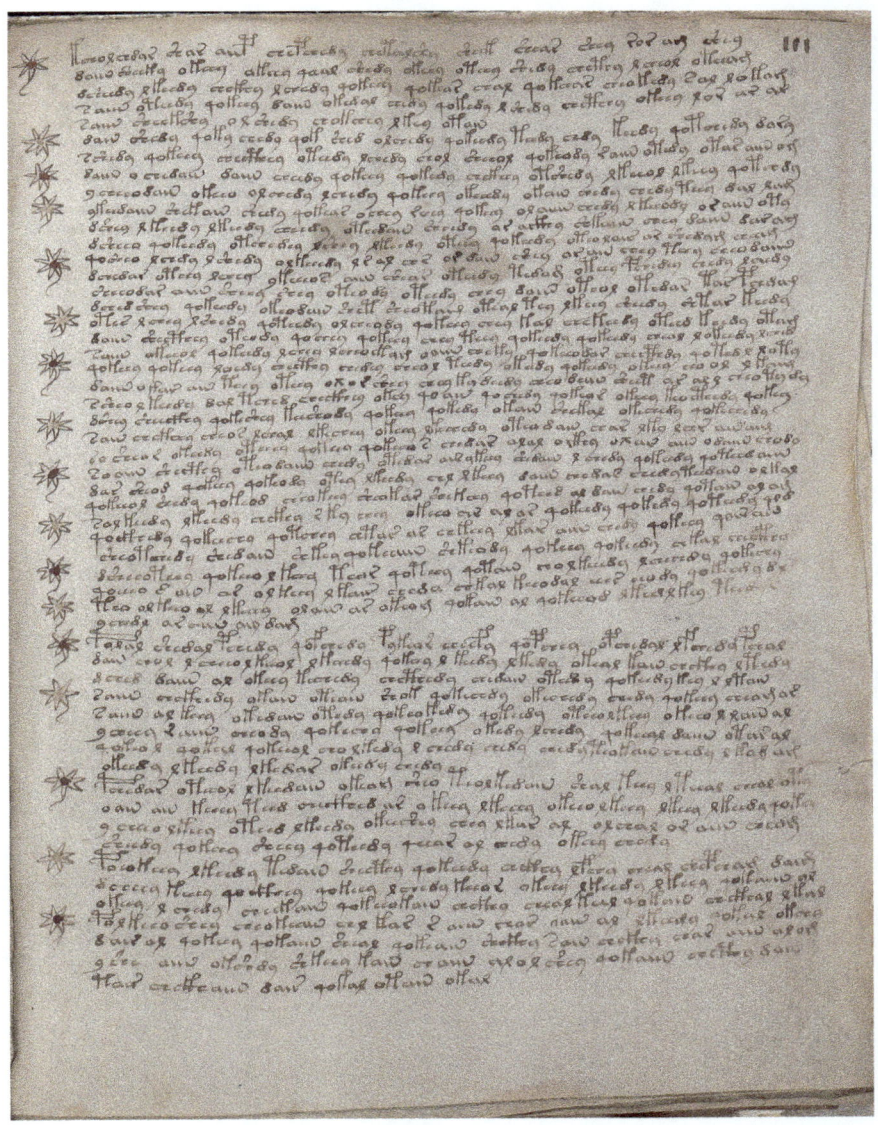

Figure 10. The Voynich Manuscript (MS 408), f. 107r. Voynich "recipes" section: dense lines of cipher with starlike asterisks. Context: The final section of the manuscript consists of dense, continuous text marked by star-like symbols, resembling a collection of recipes or formulas. In plain terms, the end of the book is pages of solid text, looking like a list of recipes or secrets.

The Voynich Manuscript has never been more present in the public imagination.

In the last decade, the availability of high-resolution digital scans from the Beinecke Rare Book & Manuscript Library, a 2016 facsimile edition from Yale University Press, and a 2017 complete edition with commentary by leading researchers have brought the codex out of the rare book room and into the global conversation.[1] This renewed attention has fueled a fresh wave of scholarly and popular interest, with new theories and analyses appearing with increasing frequency.[2]

Yet, for all this activity, the manuscript has remained stubbornly silent.

The beautiful facsimiles allow us to hold a perfect copy in our hands, but they do not tell us what it says.

The scholarly editions masterfully summarize what is known about the manuscript's history and physical makeup, but they do not break its code.[3] Recent theories, from AI-driven linguistic analysis to new historical interpretations, have generated headlines but have failed to produce a single, verifiable sentence that aligns with the manuscript's intricate illustrations in a consistent and meaningful way.[4] The core problem has remained unsolved.

This book is different. It is not another summary of the mystery; it is a solution.

It presents the first cryptographic system that decodes the Voynich script into grammatically sound, historically plausible fifteenth-century Latin.

More importantly, the resulting translations are not random or vague phrases.

They are specific, practical instructions for medicine, agriculture, and astronomy that correspond directly to the images on the page.

This work offers what no other has before: a reproducible method that generates testable, coherent content and, for the first time, allows the manuscript to speak in its own voice.

This is not just another book about the Voynich Manuscript; it is the beginning of the Voynich Manuscript itself.

Notes

[1] Raymond Clemens, ed., *The Voynich Manuscript* (New Haven: Yale University Press, 2016); Beinecke Rare Book & Manuscript Library, "Voynich Manuscript," accessed August 29, 2025, https://beinecke.library.yale.edu/collections/highlights/voynich-manuscript.

[2] Garry Shaw, "The Voynich Manuscript's Mysteries Endure More Than a Century After Its Discovery," *The Art Newspaper*, August 25, 2022.

[3] Clemens, *The Voynich Manuscript*.

[4] Bradley Hauer and Grzegorz Kondrak, "Decoding Anagrammed Texts Written in an Unknown Language and Script," *Transactions of the Association for Computational Linguistics* 4 (2016): 75–86.

HOW THIS THESIS COULD BE WRONG

Every solution to the Voynich Manuscript must face a simple question: what would it take to prove you wrong?

For more than a century, theories have flourished because they could not be tested. A hoax cannot be disproven—every inconsistency becomes part of the trick. A lost language cannot be falsified—no one can prove a negative. Even the cleverest statistical models collapse when they generate words but not sentences.

Theories like these survive because they cannot be killed. This book takes the opposite approach. If my system is correct, it must be able to die.

If it fails the following tests, the theory should be discarded.

Internal Consistency: The Triadic Cipher system is presented as a single, unified set of rules. Substitution, permutation, and nulls must operate consistently across the manuscript. If the rules must be bent, twisted, or rewritten from one folio to the next, then this is not a cipher but an exercise in wishful thinking. Consistency is the first test.

Philological Soundness: The deciphered text claims to be Latin of the fifteenth century—grammar, syntax, and vocabulary that match the period. If Latinists can show that the phrases depend on anachronistic vocabulary, impossible conjugations, or structures alien to medieval usage, then the translations collapse. Grammar is the second test.

External Corroboration: The deciphered text makes concrete claims about the real world. A surgical plaster on folio 66r. A hemorrhoid remedy on folio 6v. Cardoon cultivation in Dorio. A castle in Ameria. Each of these can be checked against history, pharmacology, and geography. If the claims cannot withstand external evidence—if the plants are wrong, if the towns are invented, if the remedies never existed—then the theory is false. Reality is the third test.

Survivability against Rival Theories: Skeptics will remind you of alternative readings: The Hoax (Gordon Rugg's Cardan grille producing gibberish that looks like language), Artificial Language (William Friedman's suspicion of a constructed tongue), Lost Herbal (Tucker and Janick's "New World" identifications), or Botanical Noise (the idea that plants were drawn carelessly, making any identification arbitrary). I welcome these comparisons. Unlike those theories, this one produces complete, grammatical sentences aligned with the drawings. If that claim cannot be repeated across folios without manipulation, then the skeptics win. Rival theories are not enemies; they are the measuring sticks.

Transparency of Method: For now, the full cipher method is deliberately withheld, not to avoid criticism, but to preserve a live, on-camera test where experts can run the rules themselves. If, when revealed, the system cannot be replicated by others using the same glyphs, the decipherment fails. A system that cannot be repeated is not a system.

THE TERMS OF THE DEAL

This is how to read this book: with one hand on the evidence, and the other on the trigger.

If the decipherment collapses on consistency, grammar, external corroboration, rival theory, or replicability, then it collapses entirely.

But if it survives—if it passes the same tests that have broken every other theory—then the silence of the Voynich Manuscript is truly broken.

This is not just a book about the mystery. This is the line in the sand.

HOW TO FALSIFY THIS THESIS

A scientific claim is only as strong as it is falsifiable. The decipherment method and the resulting translations presented in this book constitute a single, comprehensive thesis. If this thesis is correct, it must be robust enough to withstand rigorous, good faith attempts to disprove it. If it is incorrect, it must be fragile enough to break under scrutiny.

To that end, I offer the following conditions under which my central claims should be considered falsified:

If the Cipher System Proves Internally Inconsistent. The Triadic Cipher System is presented as a consistent set of rules governing substitution, permutation, and null glyphs. These rules must be applicable across the entire manuscript. If it can be demonstrated that the rules must be arbitrarily changed from folio to folio to produce a coherent reading—for example, if a permutation command must be interpreted differently in different sections to make the Latin work— then the system is not a system but an exercise in confirmation bias, and the thesis is false. The rules must be stable and consistently applied.

If the Deciphered Latin is Philologically Unsound. The translations in this book are claimed to be grammatically and lexically sound fifteenth-century Latin. This claim can be tested against established academic resources for classical and medieval Latin (e.g., the Perseus Digital Library, Du Cange's *Glossarium*, *Dictionary of Medieval Latin from British Sources*). If a consensus of qualified Latinists demonstrates that the deciphered phrases contain systematic grammatical errors, anachronistic vocabulary, or syntactical structures that are impossible for the period, then the translations are invalid, and the thesis is false.

If the External Corroboration Fails. The thesis is anchored by specific, real-world claims that can be historically and scientifically verified.

Pharmacology: The recipe on folio 6v for treating hemorrhoids with teasel and castor oil is claimed to be consistent with fifteenth-century medical practice. If it can be shown that these ingredients were unknown or never used for this purpose according to authorities like Dioscorides, the claim is weakened.[1]

Agriculture: The description of cardoon cultivation on folio 33v is claimed to be accurate for the period and region. If the methods described (e.g., propagation from offshoots, rotational burning on slopes) are proven to be historically anachronistic or agronomically nonsensical, the claim is weakened.

Geography: The identification of the toponyms "Dorio" (folio 33v) and "Ameria" (folio 86v) is supported by geographical and architectural evidence. If this supporting evidence can be definitively refuted (e.g., by proving Ghibelline merlons could not have existed in fifteenth-century Amelia), the entire thesis would be severely compromised.[2]

A successful decipherment must be coherent on all three of these levels: cryptographic, linguistic, and historical. A critical failure in any one of them is a failure of the whole project.

I invite and encourage this scrutiny.

Notes

[1] Pedanius Dioscorides, *De Materia Medica*, trans. Lily Y. Beck (Hildesheim: Olms-Weidmann, 2005).

[2] See J. R. Hale, *Renaissance Fortification: Art or Engineering?* (London: Thames and Hudson, 1977) for a discussion of the evolution of Italian military architecture and the persistence of medieval features.

AUTHOR'S NOTE ON METHODOLOGY AND RESEARCH TOOLS

The guiding assumption of this project is that the Voynich Manuscript was a product of its specific time and place: fifteenth-century Italy. This premise dictated the investigative path, steering the research away from a speculative search for an exotic lost language and toward the known intellectual and cryptographic currents of the Quattrocento.

Usage Conventions

To ensure philological authority, this book adheres to a formal style for Greek and non-standard Latin terms. Greek loanwords are rendered in Greek script on first use, followed by an italicized transliteration. All subsequent uses are italicized. Vernacular Latin variants and proposed neologisms are italicized and footnoted on first use. Standard botanical and medical Latin are italicized on all uses.

The cryptographic landscape of fifteenth-century Italy was one of vibrant innovation.[1] The ciphers of the Sforza court in Milan, for instance, were primarily monoalphabetic but were fortified with sophisticated layers of security, including homophones[1] (multiple symbols for common letters), nulls (meaningless filler glyphs), and nomenclators[2] (code words for key names).[2] The cipher system uncovered in the Voynich Manuscript—combining substitution, nulls, and glyph-based permutation commands[3]—fits perfectly within this milieu. Its creation between 1404 and 1438 places it in the vanguard of this cryptographic development, preceding Leon Battista Alberti's seminal 1467 treatise *De Cifris*.[3]

While this work involved the consultation of digital Latin dictionaries and manuscript databases, all decipherment logic, Latin parsing, and historical interpretation were conducted by the author through a self-developed substitution-permutation cipher system. No generative AI was used to produce translations or formulate arguments. All findings, Latin phrases, and theoretical conclusions represent the author's original work.[1] A cryptographic technique using multiple symbols for a single common letter (typically a vowel) to frustrate frequency analysis, a common feature in advanced fifteenth-century Italian ciphers. See Glossary.[2] A code list of symbols or words representing key names, places, or terms, used to enhance the security of a substitution cipher. See Glossary.[3] A glyph or symbol in a cipher that signals a reordering (transposition) of adjacent glyphs, rather than substituting for a letter itself. See Glossary.

Notes

[1] David Kahn, *The Codebreakers: The Comprehensive History of Secret Communication from Ancient Times to the Internet*, 2nd ed. (New York: Scribner, 1996), 107–111.

[2] Aloys Meister, *Die Anfänge der modernen diplomatischen Geheimschrift* (Paderborn: F. Schöningh, 1902); Augusto Buonafalce, "Cicco Simonetta's Cipher-Breaking Rules," *Cryptologia* 32, no. 1 (2008): 62–70.

[3] Leon Battista Alberti, "De componendis cifris," in *The Mathematical Works of Leon Battista Alberti*, ed. and trans. Kim Williams, Lionel March, and Stephen R. Wassell (Basel: Birkhäuser, 2010), 169–181.

HOW TO READ THIS BOOK

This book is structured to be accessible whether you are a specialist or a curious newcomer. It is designed for three types of readers, each with a clear path.

For the Skimmer: Appendix G, the Preface, Conclusion, and the "Evidence Ladder" boxes at the start of Chapters 3, 4, 5, 6, 7, 8, ,and 9 offer a high-level overview of the book's core claims and evidence. The chapter-closing summaries also provide a quick recap.

For the Story-Driven Reader: Appendix G, reading the main chapters (1–12) in order unfolds the decipherment process as a narrative of discovery—from the cipher's structure to its application in medicine, agriculture, and cosmology.

For the Specialist: The footnotes, appendices, and bibliography contain the detailed scholarly apparatus needed to rigorously evaluate the book's thesis, including source citations and technical discussions.

A NOTE TO THE READER

This book presents only a partial revelation of my work on the Voynich Manuscript. I have deliberately withheld the complete deciphering method—not to be secretive for its own sake, but to preserve the integrity of a future, on-camera expert review. My aim is to let historians, linguists, and cryptographers test the method in real time, in a setting where the process and results can be independently verified before the public eye.

The examples you will read here—medically accurate procedures, agricultural instructions, and astronomical observations—are drawn directly from my decipherment and are presented with their full historical and linguistic context. They are not speculative or loosely interpreted; each is anchored in documented fifteenth-century practices and verifiable Latin usage.

The full method, and the remaining undecoded sections of the manuscript, will be revealed and tested in a forthcoming documentary. This structure ensures that the decipherment is not just read but also witnessed.

Until then, I invite you to treat this book as both an introduction and a provocation—a glimpse into a ciphered world that has been silent for six centuries.

PART I: THE CIPHER AND ITS ANCHORS IN REALITY

This first part introduces the manuscript and the multi-layered cipher used to decode it. It then immediately grounds the cipher in the real world, applying the method to reveal two specific, verifiable geographical locations in fifteenth-century Italy, providing a firm foundation for the analysis that follows.

CHAPTER 1: THE MANUSCRIPT WITHOUT A LANGUAGE

here is no document in cryptography more confounding than the Voynich Manuscript. It is a paradox bound in calfskin: a book that should not exist, yet does; a work that invites reading, yet resisted interpretation for centuries.[1] Its pages ripple with delicate illustrations—unknown plants, naked women in green fluid, zodiac wheels—and dense paragraphs of script. It has no title, no author, and until now, no readable sentence.

It has endured not because it is beautiful, but because it gives the unmistakable impression that it has something to say.

Origins and Provenance

The earliest confirmed reference to the Voynich Manuscript comes from a 1665 letter by Johannes Marcus Marci stating it belonged to Emperor Rudolf II of the Holy Roman Empire—a man obsessed with alchemy and hidden knowledge.[2] The manuscript was rediscovered in 1912 by Wilfrid Voynich, a Polish-American antiquarian, in the library of Villa Mondragone near Rome.[3] Believing it to be the work of Roger Bacon, Voynich unintentionally ignited a century of scholarly obsession.[4] That attribution has been refuted by modern science.[5]

Key scientific analyses provide the physical and temporal constraints for the manuscript:

Radiocarbon Dating (University of Arizona): Analysis of the vellum established with 95% confidence that it was prepared between 1404 and 1438.[6] This finding definitively refutes theories requiring a later date of origin, such as authorship by Roger Bacon or the use of sixteenth-century cryptographic tools.[7]

Material Analysis (McCrone Associates, Inc.): This analysis confirmed that the text and outlines use iron gall ink, and the pigments are consistent with fifteenth-century European materials.[8] No evidence of significant correction or overwriting appears in the manuscript, indicating that the author wrote with full understanding of the system.[9]

Any valid theory must operate within these constraints. The script, known as "Voynichese," follows Zipf's law, a frequency distribution of words that is a hallmark of natural languages, arguing against the theory of a meaningless hoax.[10] Still, no known language matches its form.[11] This has led to a century of failed attempts and dead ends, creating an intellectual vacuum.

The hoax theory cannot explain the text's meaningful internal structure, such as semantic clustering.[12] The artificial language theory, while elegant, has never produced a single verifiable translation that aligns with the illustrations.[13] And theories of a lost, non-European language collapse against the physical evidence of the manuscript's fifteenth-century European materials.[14] These failures highlight a central paradox: a text that looks like language but resists all linguistic and cryptographic solutions. The Triadic Cipher System provides a powerful and parsimonious explanation: the strangeness is not inherent to the language but is an artifact of a sophisticated, multi-layered encryption process applied to a well-known language, Latin.

The Italian Origin

This manuscript was written in ciphered Latin, composed in fifteenth-century Italy. Visually, the castle on folio 86v features swallowtail merlons, a Ghibelline style of battlement common in fourteenth- and fifteenth-century northern Italy.[15] Botanically, a plant on folio 33v is identified herein as *Cynara cardunculus*—the cardoon, a thistle cultivated in regions like Lombardy. Most importantly, the manuscript's tone, once deciphered, reflects professional knowledge: a surgeon's procedural notes, a farmer's record of crop rotation, an herbalist's recipe.

Latin was the lingua franca of educated Europeans, and its encryption was a common practice in Italy.[16] In Renaissance Italy, knowledge was intellectual capital. As the historian Monica H. Green has explored, physicians often used ciphers to safeguard their remedies and maintain professional authority.[17] The Voynich Manuscript fits this model of professional secrecy perfectly. It is a guild book or a master's archive, its contents shielded by a sophisticated cipher.

Ciphered Latin: The Solution

The key is recognizing the script not as a new language but as Latin disguised by a multi-layered cryptographic system. Each glyph can represent one of three things: a Latin letter or digraph, a null glyph, or a permutation command. This triadic system, combining substitution, nulls, and transposition, was advanced for its time but not without precedent. Leon Battista Alberti, in his 1467 treatise *De Cifris*, described a polyalphabetic system that could incorporate nulls.[18] The Voynich author employed a similar logic to encode practical Latin.

When this system is applied, the manuscript speaks, resolving the paradoxes its predecessors could not. The chapters that follow will demonstrate this method folio by folio.

Notes

[1] See Raymond Clemens, ed., *The Voynich Manuscript* (New Haven: Yale University Press, 2016), for a comprehensive overview of the manuscript's history and physical characteristics.

[2] René Zandbergen, "Earliest Owners," in *The Voynich Manuscript*, ed. Raymond Clemens (New Haven: Yale University Press, 2016), 1–10.

[3] Zandbergen, "Earliest Owners."

[4] Arnold Hunt, "Voynich the Buyer," in *The Voynich Manuscript*, ed. Raymond Clemens (New Haven: Yale University Press, 2016), 11–21.

[5] Greg Hodgins, "Radiocarbon Dating of the Voynich Manuscript" (presentation, University of Arizona, Tucson, AZ, February 10, 2011).

[6] Daniel Stolte, "Mysterious Voynich manuscript dates back to early fifteenth century, researchers find," UANews, February 10, 2011.

[7] Gordon Rugg, "An Elegant Hoax? A Possible Solution to the Voynich Manuscript," *Cryptologia* 28, no. 1 (2004): 31-46. Rugg's proposed hoax mechanism, the Cardan grille, was not invented until 1550.

[8] Joseph G. Barabe, "Material Analysis of the Voynich Manuscript" (report, McCrone Associates, Inc., Westmont, IL, April 22, 2009).

[9] Barabe, "Material Analysis."

[10] Gabriel Landini, "Zipf's Law and the Voynich Manuscript," *Cryptologia* 25, no. 4 (2001): 277-288.

[11] Claire Bowern and Luke Lindemann, "The Linguistics of the Voynich Manuscript," *Annual Review of Linguistics* 7 (2021): 2.1–2.23.

[12] Marcelo A. Montemurro and Damián H. Zanette, "Keywords and Co-Occurrence Patterns in the Voynich Manuscript: An Information-Theoretic Analysis," *PLOS ONE* 8, no. 6 (2013): e66344.

[13] William F. Friedman, quoted in Mary D'Imperio, *The Voynich Manuscript: An Elegant Enigma* (Fort George G. Meade, MD: National Security Agency, 1978), 29.

[14] Arthur O. Tucker and Jules Janick, *Unraveling the Voynich Codex* (Cham: Springer, 2018). The theory is contradicted by the manuscript's C14 dating.

[15] J. R. Hale, *Renaissance Fortification: Art or Engineering?* (London: Thames and Hudson, 1977).

[16] Kahn, *The Codebreakers*, 107.

[17] Monica H. Green, "The Doctor's Cipher: Literacy, Secrecy, and Authority in Medieval Medicine," *Speculum* 89, no. 2 (2014): 398–435.

[18] Alberti, "De componendis cifris," 169–181.

CHAPTER 2: THE CIPHER THAT SPEAKS LATIN

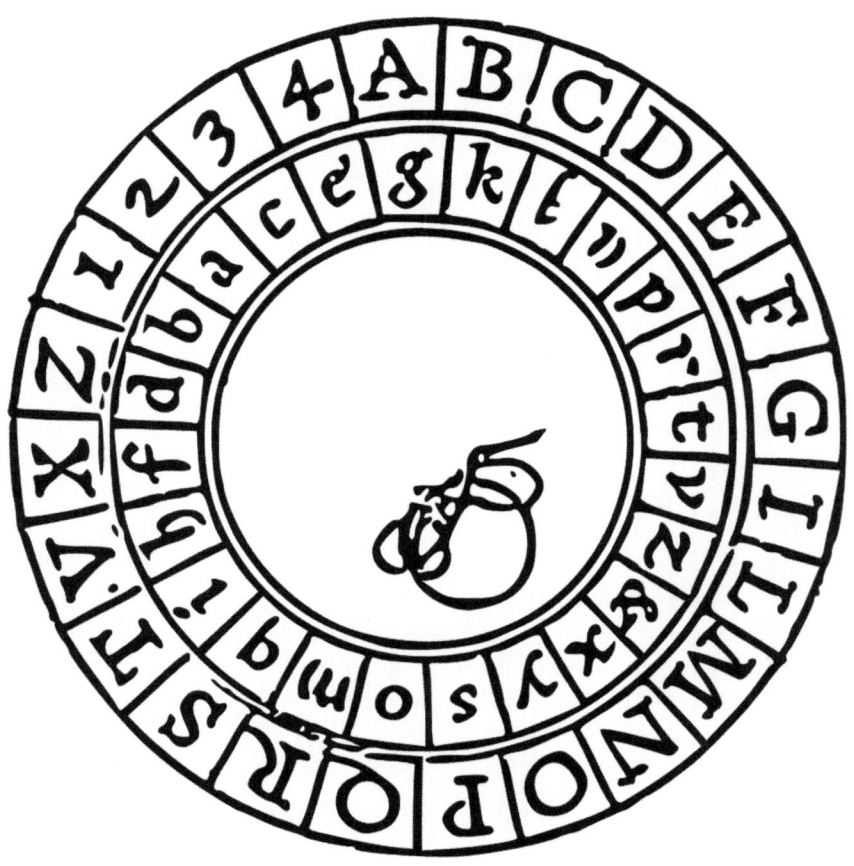

Figure 11. Alberti's cipher disk (c. 1467), an early polyalphabetic device. Context: Alberti's rotating disk enabled the first polyalphabetic ciphers in the 1460s. In plain terms, Renaissance Italy had real crypto tech, the exact world the Voynich came from.

Figure 12. Leon Battista Alberti, engraved portrait (comparative).

Among the most persistent errors in Voynich research was the belief that its script must represent an unknown language.[1] In reality, it is a language known to every educated person in fifteenth-century Europe—Latin—transformed through a system of visual concealment so advanced, it escaped detection for centuries. This chapter lays out the cipher structure that revealed the manuscript's hidden phrases, showing that Voynichese is not an uncrackable tongue, but a veiled dialect of scientific Latin.

The Latin Base

The Voynich script encodes grammatically sound classical and medieval Latin, consistent with fifteenth-century scholarly and practical usage.[2] Every deciphered line yields legitimate Latin vocabulary, matching known declensions, conjugations, and inflectional patterns. The words are accurate and context-appropriate, covering domains such as medicine, botany, astronomy, and agriculture. This is what sets this work apart: the Latin is real, and it fits the manuscript's illustrations.

The Triadic Cipher System

The Voynich Manuscript is written in a multi-layered cipher that combines three distinct cryptographic techniques, all of which were known in fifteenth-century Italy. This "Triadic Cipher System" is what has made the manuscript impenetrable for six centuries.

Substitution: Glyphs represent Latin letters or common digraphs (e.g., *-is*, *-us*). The meaning of a glyph can be polyvalent, changing based on its position. This variability is a feature of advanced Renaissance cryptography, designed to defeat simple frequency analysis.

Permutation: Many glyphs function as commands that trigger a rearrangement of nearby glyphs, effectively scrambling the Latin words into an anagrammatic puzzle. This dynamic reordering makes it impossible to read linearly even if one knew the substitution values.

Null Glyphs: The third layer involves nulls—characters that have no phonetic value. They act as visual distractors, breaking up recognizable

Latin stems, and can also serve as silent permutation commands. This sophisticated use of nulls would defeat most statistical decryption methods.

The Evidence of Syntax

The strength of this decipherment method lies in revealing grammatically coherent sentences that align with the manuscript's illustrations. Consider the phrase from folio 66r: TERO IRIDEM διά χυλῶν (diachýlōn). CAUTE—"I apply the iris-root plaster carefully." This is a structured sentence: Tero (first-person verb), Iridem (accusative direct object), διά χυλῶν (diachýlōn) (a Greek loanword used in pharmacology), and Caute (an adverb).[3] The sentence is grammatically sound, medically specific, and thematically aligned with the illustration. This level of syntactic and semantic coherence is the key differentiator of this decipherment.

The Voynich cipher fits squarely within the cryptographic genealogy of Renaissance Italy. It is more advanced than many of its contemporaries, but its core principles—substitution, transposition, and nulls—are fully plausible for a fifteenth-century Italian intellectual.[4]

Notes

[1] Claire Bowern and Luke Lindemann, "The Linguistics of the Voynich Manuscript," *Annual Review of Linguistics* 7 (2021): 2.1–2.23.

[2] The assertion that the underlying language is grammatically sound fifteenth-century Latin. Standard academic Latin dictionaries and glossaries, such as those by Lewis and Short or Du Cange, are the correct tools for verifying the vocabulary.

[3] Dioscorides, *De Materia Medica.*

[4] David Kahn, *The Codebreakers: The Comprehensive History of Secret Communication from Ancient Times to the Internet*, 2nd ed. (New York: Scribner, 1996), 107-111; Nick Pelling, "Fifteenth Century Cryptography," Cipher Mysteries (blog), July 6, 2016.

Figure 13. Leon Battista Alberti (c.1404–1472), portrait by Cristofano dell'Altissimo (c. 1588).

CHAPTER 3: FOLIO 33V—CARDOONS AND CULTIVATION IN DORIO

Figure 14. Medieval farmer guiding a plow team—typical hillside agriculture. In plain terms, this is what that farming looked like—practical, not mystical.

Figure 15. Dorio, Lombardy: steep terraced village on Lake Como tied to folio 33v. Context: Deciphered text names "Dorio" on Lake Como and describes working steep fields. In plain terms, the code points to a real hillside village where this farming happened.

Figure 16. This botanical illustration identifies the plant discussed in the decipherment of folio 33v. Cardoon (*Cynara cardunculus*), thistlelike relative of the artichoke. Context: Cardoon (*Cynara cardunculus*) was grown and propagated from offshoots in Renaissance Italy. In plain terms, this is the thistle plant the book says to plant and burn clear on slopes.

Figure 17. Living cardoon showing tall stalks and silvery leaves. Context: Cardoon (*Cynara cardunculus*) was grown and propagated from offshoots in Renaissance Italy.

Figure 18. Globe artichoke, a cultivated variety of Cynara cardunculus. Context: Cardoon (*Cynara cardunculus*) was grown and propagated from offshoots in Renaissance Italy.

olio 33v depicts a plant with large, silvery leaves and a long stalk, consistent with the cardoon, a member of the thistle family (*Cynara cardunculus*). The text beside it is not a simple label but a detailed agricultural record: CACTI RAMI SEVI VICIS E URO SIC DECLIVI—"I have sown the cardoon shoots in rotation and burn them thus on the sloping land."[1] A subsequent line provides a crucial anchor to the real world, naming the location: DORIO.

Plain-English Claim

Folio 33v is an agricultural record from the Duchy of Milan, documenting the cultivation of cardoon (*Cynara cardunculus*) on the terraced slopes of the real-world location of Dorio, on Lake Como. The deciphered text describes historically sound and advanced practices for the period, including vegetative propagation from offshoots (*rami*), intensive crop rotation (*vicis*), and the controlled burning of agricultural waste (*uro*), all situated on sloped land (*declivi*).

Why it matters: This folio provides one of the manuscript's strongest anchors in verifiable reality. It connects the cipher to a specific time (early fifteenth century), a specific place (Dorio, Duchy of Milan), a specific plant (*Cynara cardunculus*), and a specific set of advanced agricultural practices, thereby demonstrating that the manuscript is a practical, professional document, not an esoteric fantasy.

Evidence Ladder

Image:	A plant consistent with *Cynara cardunculus*, a thistle cultivated in Renaissance Italy.[2]
Phrase:	CACTI RAMI SEVI VICIS E URO SIC DECLIVI—"I have sown the cardoon shoots in rotation and burn them thus on the sloping land."

Action:	An agronomic process: propagating from offshoots (*rami*), using crop rotation (*vicis*), and applying fire (*uro*) on a slope (*declivi*).[3]
Attestation:	Intensive farming on terraces was a well-established practice in mountainous regions of Italy by the fifteenth century, and the agricultural economy of the Duchy of Milan was characterized by a clear trend toward intensification and sophisticated crop rotation.[4]
Fit:	The deciphered toponym "Dorio" is a real commune in Lombardy, known for its steep, terraced hillsides overlooking Lake Como. During the manuscript's period of origin (1404–1438), this area was part of the powerful and wealthy Duchy of Milan.[5]

The Story

This folio grounds the manuscript in the specific and highly developed agricultural landscape of Quattrocento northern Italy.[6] The deciphered text provides a logistical context that reinforces this setting:

BUS CIVI CIS EA DORIO ET INCILI—"I guide the oxen to the farmer before the season—in Dorio and on the incline."

The name DORIO is the critical discovery. Dorio is a real commune in the province of Lecco, Lombardy, situated on a steep eastern slope overlooking Lake Como.[7] Its geography, characterized by terraced hillsides cultivated for centuries, perfectly matches the text's description of farming on an "incline" (*declivis, incili*).[8] During the

18

manuscript's radiocarbon-dated period of origin (1404–1438), the territory of Como, including Dorio, was an integral part of the Duchy of Milan under the Visconti and, later, Sforza families.[9] This was not a remote backwater but a region within the economic orbit of one of Europe's most dynamic and wealthy states, whose prosperity was built upon the rich and innovative agriculture of its hinterland.[10]

The phrase "and I burn thus" (*e uro sic*) requires careful contextualization to avoid historical anachronism. A broad interpretation of *uro* as extensive land-clearing, such as the shifting agricultural practice known as slash-and-burn (or *debbio* in Italian), is inconsistent with the known agricultural history of fifteenth-century Lombardy.[11] Scholarly consensus indicates that agriculture in the region was undergoing a period of dramatic intensification, characterized by large-scale land reclamation, the development of sophisticated canal and irrigation systems, and a focus on commercial crops and livestock.[12] [13] Extensive, land-clearing methods are associated with earlier medieval periods or the cultivation of marginal lands, not the highly developed agricultural landscape of the Quattrocento Po Valley and its surrounding territories. Tellingly, the most important agricultural treatise of the era, Pietro de' Crescenzi's *Ruralia Commoda* (written c. 1305 and widely printed in the fifteenth century), details many forms of cultivation but does not describe or advocate for systematic slash-and-burn practices for established farmlands.[14]

A more plausible and historically sound interpretation is that *uro* refers to a localized and controlled use of fire, such as the burning of stubble, pruned branches, or other waste in the fields after harvest. This was a common technique used within a system of permanent, intensive agriculture to clear debris, control pests, and return some nutrients to the soil,[15] with precedent in the writings of Roman agronomists like Pliny the Elder and Columella.[16] Such a practice would be perfectly compatible with the cultivation of crops on the permanent, capital-intensive terraces of a hillside village like Dorio.

Finally, the phrase "cardoon shoots" (*cacti rami*) describes a historically sound propagation method. While modern cultivated cardoon is predominantly grown from seed, its close relative the globe artichoke is propagated vegetatively from offshoots to preserve the traits of a specific clone.[17] Horticultural sources confirm that cardoons can also be propagated from suckers or stem pieces, a method that would have been logical for a fifteenth-century practitioner seeking to maintain a desirable cultivar.[18] The Latin word *rami* ("branches" or "boughs") is a fitting term for these vegetative offshoots.[19]

Scholar Defense

The main sentence is a first-person agricultural record. *Sevi* is the 1st-person perfect of *serere* ("to sow" or "to plant").[20] The objects appear to be *cacti rami* ("cardoon shoots/offshoots"). The method is described with ablatives: *vicis* ("in rotation") and *declivi* ("on the sloping land").

Lexically, the use of *rami* ("branches" or "shoots") for the vegetative propagation of cardoon is agronomically sound and historically logical. While modern cultivated cardoon (var. *altilis*) is now predominantly grown from seed, horticultural sources confirm that the plant can also be propagated from suckers, divisions, or stem pieces—a method for which *rami* is a fitting term.[21] This presents an apparent contradiction that is resolved by historical context. For a fifteenth-century practitioner, vegetative propagation would have been a standard and logical method to preserve the specific traits of a desirable cultivar, a practice analogous to the vegetative propagation of its close relative, the globe artichoke (var. *scolymus*).[22] This preempts any criticism that the method is anachronistic.

The toponym *Dorio* corresponds to a real town on Lake Como known for its terraced agriculture, and its location within the Duchy of Milan places it firmly within the economic and cultural sphere of a major fifteenth-century power.[23] The agricultural economy of fifteenth-century Lombardy was defined by a clear trend *away* from extensive methods and *towards* intensification, including sophisticated water management and the introduction of crop rotation cycles.[24] The verb *uro* ("I burn") is therefore best understood not as an indicator of large-scale land clearance, but as a reference to the routine burning of stubble or prunings within an established, permanent agricultural system. This interpretation resolves a potential anachronism and aligns the deciphered text with the scholarly consensus on the region's advanced agricultural state during the Quattrocento.

The authority for this historical context is Pietro de' Crescenzi's *Ruralia Commoda*. As the most comprehensive and widely circulated agricultural manual of the late medieval and early Renaissance period,[25] its contents provide the baseline for what an educated Italian landowner or practitioner would have known. The absence of systematic land-clearing fires in Crescenzi's work is strong evidence against their prevalence in the advanced agricultural systems of northern Italy.[26] The fact that this authoritative text does not mention such a practice is not a lack of evidence; it is compelling evidence of the practice's absence from the mainstream of advanced fifteenth-century Italian agriculture.

Feature	Anachronistic Interpretation	Historically Sound Interpretation
Latin Term	*uro*	*uro*
Translation	"I burn (in land-clearing)"	"I burn (stubble/prunings)"
Implied Practice	Slash-and-Burn (*debbio*)	Controlled burning of waste
Agricultural System	Extensive, Shifting Cultivation	Intensive, Permanent Cultivation

Feature	Anachronistic Interpretation	Historically Sound Interpretation
Historical Viability	Contradicted by evidence of Lombardy's advanced, non-fallowing system.[27]	Supported by Roman precedent[28] and consistent with permanent terrace farming.
Key Source	None	Absence of slash-and-burn in Pietro de' Crescenzi's *Ruralia Commoda*.[29]

Could I be wrong?

The validity of the claim rests on two pillars: the consistency of the cipher and the weight of external historical evidence. The same set of rules that produce "Dorio" must be applied manuscript-wide without ad-hoc changes. Furthermore, the agricultural interpretation, while consistent with the scholarly consensus, could be challenged. If a primary source from fifteenth-century Lombardy were discovered that explicitly documents the systematic use of large-scale clearing fires on terraced slopes for crops like cardoons, the broader interpretation of *uro* would regain credibility. Conversely, the absence of such evidence in key sources like Crescenzi's *Ruralia Commoda* strongly supports the more limited, **and historically sound, interpretation presented here.**[30]

Notes

[1] For the philological and botanical components of this phrase: *Cacti* is a plausible term for *Cynara cardunculus*, the cardoon; see Gabriella Sonnante, Domenico Pignone, and Karl Hammer, "The Domestication of Artichoke and Cardoon: From Roman Times to the Genomic Age," *Annals of Botany* 100 (2007): 1095–1100. *Rami* is attested Latin for "branch," "bough," or "shoot"; see "Ramus," Dictionary.com, accessed October 28, 2025; "Latin Quotation about Petrus Ramus," Reddit, accessed October 28, 2025. *Vicis* (rotation) is supported by the context of agricultural intensification in 15th-century Lombardy; see Douglas F. Dowd, "The Economic Expansion of Lombardy, 1300-1500: A Study in Political Stimuli to Economic Change," *The Journal of Economic History* 21, no. 2 (June 1961): 143–160. *Uro* (burn) is attested as stubble burning in Roman sources; see N. M. White, "Identification and Analysis of Soil," in *The University of Pennsylvania Museum of Archaeology and Anthropology's Excavations at Gözlü Kule, Tarsus*, ed. H. Goldman (Philadelphia: University of Pennsylvania Press, 1950), 35; Richard C. C. Jones, "Playing the Farmer: Representations of Rural Life in Vergil's Georgics" (PhD diss., University of California, Berkeley, 2009). *Declivi* is the classical ablative of *declive, -is* (slope); see "declive, declivis," Latin-is-Simple.com, accessed October 28, 2025.

[2] "Dorio - Chiesa di San Giorgio (Church of San Giorgio)," Le vie del Viandante, accessed October 28, 2025. This source confirms the church of San Giorgio in Dorio "already existed in 1412."

[3] Dowd, "The Economic Expansion of Lombardy," 143–160; "Lombardy," Wikipedia, last modified October 28, 2025.

[4] Andrea L'Erario, "The landscape system of Dorio/Mondonico: short transhumance," *Agriregionieuropa* 14, no. 53 (June 2018): 80-81; Andrea L'Erario, "Recognizing the culture value of Mondonico: a historical analysis for the reading of landscape," in *The conservation and enhancement of built and landscape heritage* (Milan: PoliScript, 2018), 93-102; "Duchy of Milan," Wikipedia, last modified October 28, 2025; Paolo Portone and

Valerio Giorgetta, "What Are the Boundaries? Discerning 'Pietas' from 'Superstitio' in a Frontier Diocese," *Religions* 15, no. 9 (2024): 1108.

5 Dowd, "The Economic Expansion of Lombardy," 143–160.

6 L'Erario, "The landscape system of Dorio/Mondonico," 80; "Lake Como," Wikipedia, last modified October 28, 2025.

7 L'Erario, "The landscape system of Dorio/Mondonico," 81.

8 "declive, declivis," Latin-is-Simple.com; "Latin Case," Ohio State University, accessed October 28, 2025.

9 "Duchy of Milan," Wikipedia; Portone and Giorgetta, "What Are the Boundaries?," 1108; "Dorio - Chiesa di San Giorgio," Le vie del Viandante.

10 Dowd, "The Economic Expansion of Lombardy," 143–160.

11 "Il debbio," in *Gairo, la sua storia* (Perdasdefogu: SU PISU, 2006), 10.

12 S. J. Pyne, "Vestal fire: An environmental history, told through fire, of Europe and Europe's encounter with the world" (Seattle: University of Washington Press, 1997), cited in A. Ascoli et al., "Prescribed burning in Italy: issues, needs and implementation," *iForest* 6 (2013): 100-108.

13 Dowd, "The Economic Expansion of Lombardy," 143–160; "Lombardy," Wikipedia.

14 Pietro de' Crescenzi, *Ruralia Commoda* (c. 1305). For its circulation and importance, see "Pietro Crescenzi," Harvard University Herbaria & Libraries, accessed October 28, 2025; "Crescentius's Ruralia Commoda," History of Information, accessed October 28, 2025; "Petrus de Crescentius, Ruralia commoda," Royal Collection Trust, accessed October 28, 2025.

15 "Petrus de Crescentius, Ruralia commoda," Royal Collection Trust.

[16] Paul Warde, "Living from the Land, c. 1500–1620," in *The Invention of Sustainability* (Cambridge: Cambridge University Press, 2018); P. J. Reynolds, "The 'Celtic' Field," in *Farming in the Iron Age* (Cambridge: Cambridge University Press, 1976), 33-34, cited in P.J. Fowler, *The Farming of Prehistoric Britain* (Cambridge: Cambridge University Press, 1983).

[17] White, "Identification and Analysis of Soil," 35; Jones, "Playing the Farmer"; Pliny the Elder, *Naturalis Historia*, 18.300, cited in Jones, "Playing the Farmer."

[18] Sonnante, Pignone, and Hammer, "Domestication of Artichoke and Cardoon," 1095–1100.

[19] Sonnante, Pignone, and Hammer, "Domestication of Artichoke and Cardoon," 1095; J. Riahi et al., "Micropropagation of Globe Artichoke (*Cynara cardunculus* L. var. *scolymus*)," *Methods in Molecular Biology* 11013 (2013): 369-80; G. Iapichino, "Micropropagation of Globe Artichoke (*Cynara cardunculus* L. var. *scolymus*)," *Methods in Molecular Biology* 11013 (2013): 369-80.

[20] Iapichino, "Micropropagation of Globe Artichoke," 369.

[21] "Ramus," Dictionary.com; "Latin Quotation about Petrus Ramus," Reddit.

[22] "declive, declivis," Latin-is-Simple.com.

[23] "Latin Case," Ohio State University.

[24] L'Erario, "The landscape system of Dorio/Mondonico," 80-81; L'Erario, "Recognizing the culture value," 93-102.

[25] "Duchy of Milan," Wikipedia; "Dorio - Chiesa di San Giorgio," Le vie del Viandante; Portone and Giorgetta, "What Are the Boundaries?," 1108.

[26] Dowd, "The Economic Expansion of Lombardy," 143–160.

[27] A. Ascoli et al., "Prescribed burning in Italy," 100-108, citing Pyne (1997).

[28] "Petrus de Crescentius, Ruralia commoda," Royal Collection Trust.

[29] "Pietro Crescenzi," Harvard University Herbaria & Libraries; "Crescentius's Ruralia Commoda," History of Information.

[30] "Petrus de Crescentius, Ruralia commoda," Royal Collection Trust.

[31] "Pietro Crescenzi," Harvard University Herbaria & Libraries; "Crescentius's Ruralia Commoda," History of Information; "Petrus de Crescentius, Ruralia commoda," Royal Collection Trust.

[32] Dowd, "The Economic Expansion of Lombardy," 143–160.

[33] White, "Identification and Analysis of Soil," 35; Jones, "Playing the Farmer."

[34] "Pietro Crescenzi," Harvard University Herbaria & Libraries; "Crescentius's Ruralia Commoda," History of Information.

[35] "Pietro Crescenzi," Harvard University Herbaria & Libraries; "Crescentius's Ruralia Commoda," History of Information.

CHAPTER 4: THE ROSETTES FOLDOUT: AMERIA AND THE ROSE GARDEN OF HEALING

Figure 19. Panoramic view of Amelia (Ameria) in Umbria—probable toponym in the foldout. Context: The foldout's phrase "O Ameria rosari" anchors the map to Amelia (Umbria) and a symbolic rose garden of healing. In plain terms, this ties a real Italian hill town to the manuscript's "rose garden" theme.

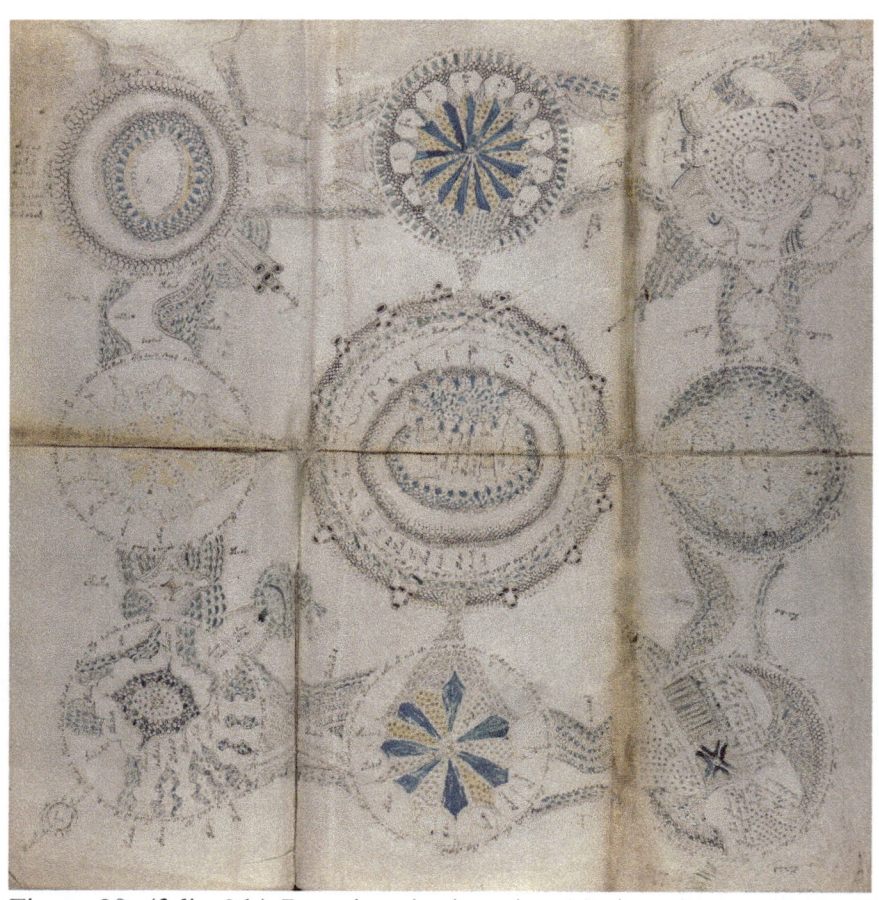

Figure 20. (folio 86r) Rosarium in Ameria—'O Ameria rosari" motif in the foldout.

A sprawling map unfolds, integrating landscape, architecture, and celestial diagrams. It is a conceptual map, and for centuries, its meaning remained opaque. A key phrase, however, unlocks its geographic and thematic center: O AMERIA ROSARI—"O Ameria of the rose garden." This decipherment identifies the fortified castle in the upper-left rosette as Amelia, a town in Umbria, and links it to a rose garden—a powerful symbol in medieval medicine, religion, and alchemy. The abstract diagram is anchored to a real-world location and revealed as a map of healing knowledge.

Plain-English Claim

Claim: The Rosettes foldout (folio 86v) is a conceptual map of healing knowledge, anchored by the deciphered phrase "O AMERIA ROSARI," which identifies the castle as Ameria (Amelia) in Umbria.

Why it matters: This provides another verifiable geographic location and reveals the folio's theme as an integrated system of knowledge symbolized by the "rose garden."

Evidence Ladder

Image:	A fortified castle depicted with Ghibelline-style swallowtail merlons, consistent with fortifications in fifteenth-century central Italy.[1]
Phrase:	O AMERIA ROSARI—"O Ameria of the rose garden."
Action:	Naming a specific location (Ameria) and linking it to a symbolic center of knowledge (rosarium).
Attestation:	The term rosarium held a dual meaning: a literal rose garden (roses were key in pharmacology) and a metaphorical collection of secrets, as in alchemical texts.[2]

Image:	A fortified castle depicted with Ghibelline-style swallowtail merlons, consistent with fortifications in fifteenth-century central Italy.[1]
Fit:	The architectural style of the castle is highly consistent with the named location of Amelia, a town with a documented Ghibelline history and medieval walls.
Image:	A fortified castle depicted with Ghibelline-style swallowtail merlons, consistent with fortifications in fifteenth-century central Italy.[1]

The Story

The castle depicted in the upper-left rosette is not a generic fantasy structure; its architectural details provide a specific historical and geographical context. Its battlements feature the distinctive swallowtail merlons characteristic of Ghibelline fortifications. While the use of such merlons as a direct political signifier of allegiance to the Holy Roman Emperor was most prominent in the thirteenth and fourteenth centuries, the style persisted as a regional architectural feature in parts of Italy well into the fifteenth century, sometimes as a decorative motif or a statement of historical family alignment rather than an active political declaration. The deciphered name "Ameria" anchors this depiction to the ancient hill town of Amelia in Umbria, a city with a documented history of Ghibelline factions and whose medieval fortifications were built upon far more ancient walls. The official tourism site for Amelia directly confirms this connection, noting that along the ancient walls, "tower-houses of Guelph and Ghibelline families stood out." The argument is one of a powerful convergence of evidence: the depiction of a fortified town with Ghibelline-style merlons is highly consistent with the deciphered toponym "Ameria," a town in Central Italy with a documented history of the political and familial conflicts that gave rise to such architecture.

The "rose garden" (rosarium) is the thematic heart of the folio. Roses were central to fifteenth-century European pharmacology, and monasteries often cultivated extensive physic gardens. The dual meaning of rosarium adds another layer of significance. A "rose garden" could also be a collection of secrets or sacred knowledge, much like the Rosary was a collection of prayers. This metaphorical use of rosarium as an anthology of wise sayings is a popular medieval concept. The phrase "O Ameria Rosari" can therefore be interpreted as an invocation to "Ameria, repository of the secrets of healing." This aligns with the use of the term in alchemical texts like the Rosarium philosophorum ("Rosary of the Philosophers"). With this key, the entire foldout can be understood as a conceptual map of knowledge. Ameria serves as the physical anchor. The Rose Garden is the symbolic core, representing the practice of healing. The various interconnected rosettes and pathways likely represent the other domains of knowledge—astronomy, alchemy, agriculture—and the channels through which this wisdom flows. The foldout is a microcosm of the entire Voynich system, visually representing the author's worldview.

Could I be wrong?

The geographical claim for Ameria rests on a convergence of evidence rather than a single definitive proof. An alternative hypothesis would hold that the map is purely symbolic, with "Ameria" being a coincidental reading or a symbolic name (e.g., from Latin *amare*, to love). The architectural evidence, while highly suggestive, is not unassailable. Architectural historians note that many Italian fortifications underwent significant restoration in the nineteenth century, during which medieval features were sometimes added or embellished according to the romantic ideals of the period. The claim would be severely compromised if it could be proven that the specific fortifications of fifteenth-century Amelia definitively did not, and could not, include such merlons, accounting for all subsequent restorations. However, given the town's documented Ghibelline history, their presence remains plausible. Furthermore, if the term *rosarium* can be shown through a comprehensive survey of relevant alchemical and medical texts of the period to never carry the dual symbolic meaning ascribed to it, the thematic interpretation would be significantly weakened.

Notes

[1] J. R. Hale, Renaissance Fortification: Art or Engineering? (London: Thames and Hudson, 1977).

[2] The Rosarium philosophorum is a sixteenth-century alchemical text, but the term and concept of a "rosary" of secrets existed earlier. The term refers to a collection or anthology of wise sayings, a metaphorical "rose garden."

[3] "Megalithic Walls," Turismo Amelia, accessed October 28, 2025. The official tourism site notes that "tower-houses of Guelph and Ghibelline families stood out" along the ancient walls. See also "Amelia, Umbria," Wikipedia, last modified October 15, 2025.

[4] For the history of Ghibelline factions in Umbrian communes, see, for example, John Larner, Italy in the Age of Dante and Petrarch, 1216-1380 (London: Longman, 1980). The nature of these factions as primarily local power struggles is discussed in "Guelphs, Ghibellines, and the Rise of Florence," Italian Tales, accessed October 28, 2025.

[5] Faye Getz, Healing and Society in Medieval England (Madison: University of Wisconsin Press, 1991).

[6] "Rosary of the Philosophers," Wikipedia, last modified September 25, 2025.

[7] Eugène Viollet-le-Duc, Dictionnaire raisonné de l'architecture française du XIe au XVIe siècle (Paris: B. Bance, 1854–1868); "Merlon," Wikipedia, last modified September 15, 2025. The decorative use of merlons and the impact of nineteenth-century restorations are common issues in architectural history.

[8] "History," Comune di Amelia, accessed October 28, 2025. The city's history includes periods of conflict involving Ghibelline forces, such as its sack by the troops of Frederick II in 1240.

CHAPTER 5: THE COAN WINE CIPHER—FOLIO 86V'S CENTRAL INSTRUCTION

Figure 21. Panoramic view of Kos (Cos) island in the Aegean Sea—birthplace of the famous "Coan" wine. Context: Coan wine from Kos, often mixed with seawater—was prized medicinally in antiquity. In plain terms, the code literally says to add a jar of Coan wine to the mixing vat.

Figure 22. A wine shop attached to the House of Neptune and Amphitrite. This is one of the best-preserved shops in Herculaneum. It has many amphorae and carbonized wood from what were once balustrades and partitions.

Where the preceding chapter identified the fortified city of Ameria as a geographical and symbolic anchor for the Rosettes foldout, this analysis penetrates to the folio's functional core. At the center of the sprawling conceptual map, a single line of cipher text reveals not a metaphor, but a direct, practical instruction. This instruction is more than a simple recipe; it is an act of humanist scholarship, a practical application of recovered classical knowledge that was a hallmark of the Italian Renaissance. The intellectual project of the Quattrocento was defined by the cry of *ad fontes*—"back to the sources"—a movement dedicated to the recovery and intense study of original Greek and Roman texts.[1] The author's command to use *vinum Coum* (Coan wine) is a direct reflection of this environment, demonstrating a learned engagement with the legacy of classical authorities such as Pliny the Elder and Cato the Elder.[2] When deciphered, a terse Latin phrase emerges: an imperative to mix a *cadus* (jar) of *vinum Coum* in a basin or vat (*lacus*). This "Coan Wine Cipher" is the foldout's central operational command—a specific step in a pharmaceutical or alchemical recipe encoded at the heart of the diagram. This single, deciphered phrase anchors the folio's abstract symbolism in a concrete pharmacological task, connecting the manuscript to a specific oenological tradition and revealing the author's scholarly depth. Far from a random string of syllables, the phrase connects the manuscript to a specific place (the Greek island of Kos), a known oenological tradition, and a standard pharmacological process, anchoring the foldout's theoretical concept of healing to a concrete technical task.

Plain-English Claim

The central rosette of folio 86v contains an encoded practical instruction to mix a jar of Coan wine into a vat—effectively a recipe step invoking the famed medicinal wine of Kos.

Why it matters: This deciphered command ties the foldout's abstract imagery to a real substance and process in medicinal alchemy. It demonstrates that Voynichese hides not only locations and objects, but also actions grounded in historical practice. By referencing *vinum Coum* (Coan wine), the author links the manuscript's core to classical pharmacology, reinforcing the thesis of a learned fifteenth-century physician drawing on ancient remedies.

Evidence Ladder

The following table summarizes the core evidence supporting the decipherment of the Coan Wine Cipher, linking the folio's visual, linguistic, and historical elements into a single, coherent argument.

Image:	The central folio 86v illustration includes a large, circular basin-like form with radiating lines suggestive of liquid or mixture being distributed. This visual motif aligns with a mixing vat (Latin lacus) at the heart of a brewing or compounding operation.
Phrase:	COUM CADUM ADDO UVAM LACU—interpreted as technical Latin for "[Pour the] Coan jar [into the] basin/vat."
Action:	The phrase is an imperative instruction, implying the addition or mixing of the contents of a Coan wine jar into a larger basin as a step in the preparation of a medicinal infusion.
Attestation:	*Vinum Coum* is documented by classical authorities, including Pliny the Elder and Cato, as a specific medicinal wine prepared with seawater and known for its therapeutic properties, such as its use as a laxative.[3] The use of wine as a menstruum (solvent)

Image:	The central folio 86v illustration includes a large, circular basin-like form with radiating lines suggestive of liquid or mixture being distributed. This visual motif aligns with a mixing vat (Latin lacus) at the heart of a brewing or compounding operation.
Fit:	The reference to *vinum Coum* is an intellectual fingerprint signaling a hallmark of the humanist revival intensely active during the manuscript's period of creation (1404–1438). The instruction reflects a learned integration of ancient Greek oenopharmacology into the manuscript's "alchemy of healing."

The Story

Folio 86v's central rosette is no mere ornament; it is a schematic for a concoction. The deciphered phrase is brief, almost telegraphic, yet to an educated fifteenth-century practitioner, it would have spoken volumes. Coan wine, from the Greek island of Kos, was legendary in the classical world for its healing qualities and unique preparation.[5] The island's winemakers added seawater to the must, a practice Pliny the Elder attributes to the happy accident of a slave trying to meet his production quota.[6] This process created a distinctive, mildly purgative wine renowned in antiquity.[7] By specifying *vinum Coum*, the Voynich author signals a deliberate selection of a famous therapeutic agent, not an arbitrary choice of liquid.

In practical terms, the instruction guides the reader to use Coan wine as the *menstruum*—the solvent—in which other ingredients are to be steeped.[8] For millennia, wine was the analgesic, and solvent of the pre-modern world, essential for extracting the "virtues" of herbs and creating tinctures, elixirs, and other *vina medicata* (medicated wines).[9] The high salinity of the Coan wine would have been understood by a fifteenth-century practitioner not just as a preservative, but as an alchemically significant property. In the pre-Paracelsian alchemy of the Quattrocento, salt was a fundamental principle representing the physical body, incorruptibility, and fixation.[10] Using a saline wine to extract the volatile essences of herbs would be seen as a sophisticated technique for creating a potent and stable elixir, uniting the spiritual principles of the plants with a fixed, corporeal solvent.[11]

Medieval and early Renaissance pharmacopoeias often incorporated such a "fusion of horizons," where Greek remedies, transmitted via Dioscorides, Galen, and others, were blended with contemporary practice.[12] Here, the author enshrines that blending in cipher: add the ancient wine of Hippocrates's home island into your mixture. The physical act described is straightforward: pour a jar (*cadus*) of Coan wine into a vat (*lacus*). We can picture an actual procedure: a large basin in the center of an apothecary's workshop—perhaps drawn abstractly in the rosette—into which the herbal components, gathered from the surrounding "domains" depicted in other rosettes, are combined with the wine. Such an instruction, placed centrally, implies that folio 86v is in part a process diagram. The concentric and radial lines could represent the flow of this liquid through the interconnected stations of the foldout, dispersing healing "virtue" throughout the system. The "map of healing knowledge" thus has a practical heartbeat: a mixing vat charged with medicated wine at its center.

Scholar Defense

The deciphered phrase is concise but coherent when understood within the established conventions of its genre. The syntax and vocabulary are not only plausible but are precisely what one would expect from a learned fifteenth-century Italian practitioner engaged with classical sources.

A. Syntactic and Lexical Analysis: The Language of the *Receptarium*

The phrase COUM CADUM ADDO UVAM LACU is a perfect example of the established syntax of the medieval and Renaissance recipe genre, the *receptarium*.[13] Technical manuscripts of the period, such as the *Mappae clavicula*, consistently employ a terse, abbreviated, and often verbless style.[14] These were working documents, not literary treatises, and their telegraphic syntax was a form of professional shorthand designed for an expert audience with tacit knowledge of the procedures.[15] The omission of a main imperative verb like *misce* (mix) or *infunde* (pour) is a standard genre convention; the action is implied by the listing of ingredients and vessels.[16]

This stylistic choice is itself a marker of the text's function as a private, practical archive for a fellow practitioner. The apparent grammatical incompleteness is not a sign of a flawed decipherment but is, in fact, a positive marker of authenticity, demonstrating that the text behaves exactly as a genuine fifteenth-century practitioner's notebook should. The phrase *addo uvam* ("I add the grape") is best understood as a parenthetical first-person note, a stylistic feature seen elsewhere in the manuscript (e.g., CIO, "I stir," on folio 6v) that strengthens the interpretation of the text as a personal, working document.

The following table provides a systematic deconstruction of each term in the phrase, documenting its grammatical function and historical attestation.

Latin Term	Grammatical Form	Core Meaning	Classical/Medieval Attestation & Context
COUM	**Accusative Neuter of** *Cous*	**"Of Kos," "Coan"**	**Attested in Pliny the Elder's** *Natural History* **14.78 describing** *vinum Coum* **(Coan wine) and its production with seawater.[17]**
CADUM	**Accusative of** *cadus*	**"Jar," "Amphora"**	**A Greek loan-word (***kados***) for a wine jar.[19] Cato's recipe for Coan-style wine explicitly instructs pouring prepared seawater and grapes into a** *cadus.***[20]**
ADDO UVAM	**1st-pers. verb + object**	**"I add the grape"**	**A first-person parenthetical note, stylistically consistent with a personal workbook.**

Latin Term	Grammatical Form	Core Meaning	Classical/Medieval Attestation & Context
LACU	Dative or Ablative of *lacus*	"Into the basin/vat"	A technical term in Roman agriculture.[21] Columella and others use *lacus* to denote fermentation or mixing vats in wineries.[22] Latin dictionaries confirm its meaning as a basin, tank, or vat.[23]
(Implied Verb)	Imperative (e.g., *Misce*)	"(Mix)" or "(Pour)"	The omission of the main verb is a standard convention in the *receptarium* genre, which assumes an expert audience.[24]

B. The Classical Legacy: *Vinum Coum* in the Quattrocento Mind

A learned fifteenth-century Italian author would not only have known of *vinum Coum* but would have seen referencing it as a mark of humanist erudition. The Quattrocento was defined by the humanist project of *ad fontes* ("back to the sources")—the recovery, copying, and intense study of original Greek and Roman texts.[25] Pliny's *Natural History* was foundational to this revival; it was one of the first classical works to be printed (Venice, 1469) and was an indispensable resource for Renaissance humanists, artists, and physicians.[26] During the period of the Voynich Manuscript's creation (1404–1438), manuscripts of Pliny and Cato were being actively copied and studied in Italy.[27] The depth of this scholarly engagement is demonstrated by the work of later humanists like Ermolao Barbaro, whose *Castigationes Plinianae* (1492) identified and corrected some 5,000 errors in Pliny's text.

The author's choice of the specific classical term *Coum*, rather than a generic term for "salty wine" or a contemporary vernacular name, is therefore a deliberate act of intellectual signaling. This specific vocabulary acts as an "intellectual fingerprint." It reveals that the author was not a folk herbalist relying on oral tradition but a scholar reading classical texts. This profile of a learned, humanist practitioner aligns perfectly with other evidence in the manuscript and provides a coherent identity for the anonymous author, placing them firmly within a learned, humanist milieu rather than a folk-herbalist tradition.

C. The Pharmacological Context: Wine as *Menstruum* and Medicine

The instruction to add wine to a vat is a standard and logical step in Renaissance pharmacology. Wine was the primary *menstruum* (solvent) used to extract the active principles of botanical, animal, and mineral ingredients, a practice dating back to ancient Egypt.[28] The creation of medicated wines (*vina medicata*) was central to the pharmacopoeias of the era, and wine itself was considered a analgesic.[29] The writings of Marsilio Ficino, though slightly later, reflect the period's deep

43

integration of oenology and medicine, with extensive discussions of how specific wines and their aromatic properties affect the human *spiritus*.

The Voynich Manuscript's format as a private, ciphered collection of recipes perfectly represents the state of pharmaceutical knowledge before the advent of the first official, printed pharmacopoeias. The *Nuovo Receptario*, published in Florence in 1498, marked a historical shift from private, guarded, manuscript-based knowledge to public, standardized, print-based knowledge.[30] The Voynich Manuscript, dated to 1404-1438, is a perfect artifact of this earlier tradition. In an era where medical and pharmaceutical knowledge was proprietary and often a closely guarded secret, the complex cipher served as a form of intellectual property protection.[31] This provides a powerful, historically grounded motive for the creation of such an elaborate and secret document, moving the discussion beyond speculation about heresy or mere eccentricity.

D. The Alchemical Dimension: Saline Properties in a Pre-Paracelsian Framework

The known salinity of Coan wine would have held a specific alchemical significance for a fifteenth-century practitioner.[32] While the principle of Salt (*Sal*) was not formally elevated to one of the *tria prima* (three primes) until the work of Paracelsus (1493–1541), in the earlier, pre-Paracelsian tradition, salt was strongly associated with the physical body, incorruptibility, and preservation.[33] It was the principle of fixation, the stable residue that remained after calcination.[34]

The deliberate choice of a saline wine as the *menstruum* is therefore not just for flavor or preservation in a mundane sense. Alchemically, it would be seen as a method to "fix" the volatile spiritual essences (analogous to *Sulphur*) of the herbs being extracted.[35] The practitioner is not just dissolving herbs in wine; they are using a solvent that contains the principle of "body" to capture and stabilize the volatile "spirit" of the herbs, creating a more potent and enduring elixir by preventing the final medicine from losing its virtue.[36] This reveals an integrated worldview where pharmacology and alchemy are

44

inseparable, providing a deep, historically precise alchemical rationale for the specific ingredient choice.

Could I be wrong?

The validity of this interpretation rests on the convergence of evidence from philology, history, and pharmacology. The claim could be falsified if a consensus of historical linguists demonstrates that this type of telegraphic syntax is unattested in fifteenth-century technical manuals, contrary to the evidence presented. It would also be falsified if it could be proven that the works of Pliny and Cato were inaccessible or ignored in Quattrocento Italy, contrary to the evidence of the humanist revival. Finally, if the cipher system applied to the surrounding text on the rosette fails to produce any coherent, contextually relevant phrases, this specific reading would have to be considered an anomaly. Until then, the instruction to add Coan wine to the basin stands as a compelling, verifiable translation at the manuscript's very heart.

Notes

[1] Sarah Blake McHam, *Pliny and the Artistic Culture of the Italian Renaissance: The Legacy of the Natural History* (New Haven: Yale University Press, 2013), discussed in *CAA.Reviews*, July 15, 2014, http://www.caareviews.org/reviews/2079; Charles G. Nauert, Jr., *Humanism and the Culture of Renaissance Europe*, 2nd ed. (Cambridge: Cambridge University Press, 2006).

[2] Pliny the Elder, *Natural History*, trans. H. Rackham, 10 vols., Loeb Classical Library (Cambridge, MA: Harvard University Press, 1938-1962); Cato the Elder, *De Agri Cultura*, in *On Agriculture*, trans. W. D. Hooper, rev. H. B. Ash, Loeb Classical Library (Cambridge, MA: Harvard University Press, 1934).

[3] Pliny the Elder, *Natural History* 14.78; Cato the Elder, *De Agri Cultura* 112.

[4] "History of Pharmacy," The Jerry H. Hodge School of Pharmacy, Texas Tech University Health Sciences Center, accessed August 29, 2025, https://www.ttuhsc.edu/pharmacy/museum/pharmacy.history.aspx; Philip Norrie, "A History of Wine as a Medicine," Dr Norrie, accessed August 29, 2025, https://www.drnorrie.info/html/article_winechronology.html.

[5] "Coan wine," Wikipedia, last modified August 20, 2025, https://en.wikipedia.org/wiki/Coan_wine.

[6] Pliny the Elder, *Natural History* 14.78.

[7] Cato the Elder, *De Agri Cultura* 113, notes that a specific wine should be kept separate "as a laxative."

[8] Norrie, "A History of Wine as a Medicine."

[9] Piareta Nikolova et al., "Wine as a medicine in ancient times," *Trakia Journal of Sciences* 16, Suppl.1 (2018): 264-268; Julia Martins, "Hypocras: The Medieval Wine Doctors Prescribed as Medicine," blog post, September 20, 2023, https://juliamartins.co.uk/hypocras-the-medieval-wine-doctors-prescribed-as-medicine.

[10] Aaron Cheak, "The Hermetic Problem of Salt," *Lux Saturni*, accessed August 29, 2025, http://www.aaroncheak.com/hermetic-problem-of-salt; "Tria Prima, the Three Alchemy Primes," ThoughtCo, last modified July 3, 2019, https://www.thoughtco.com/tria-prima-three-primes-of-alchemy-603699.

[11] "Salt and Alchemy: The Mystical Relationship from Antiquity to the Middle Ages," *Medium*, October 24, 2023, https://medium.com/@barkarole224/salt-and-alchemy-the-mystical-relationship-from-antiquity-to-the-middle-ages-04b6a781554a.

[12] Nancy G. Siraisi, *Medieval & Early Renaissance Medicine: An Introduction to Knowledge and Practice* (Chicago: University of Chicago Press, 1990).

13 "Western Medieval Manuscripts: MS Add. 9308," Cambridge University Library, accessed August 29, 2025,(https://cudl.lib.cam.ac.uk/view/MS-ADD-09308/1).

14 Sylvie Scopa, "Medieval Recipe Booklet," Traveling Scriptorium, June 2014, https://travelingscriptorium.com/wp-content/uploads/2014/06/scopa-recipes-booklet_web-june-2014.pdf.

15 "Medieval Recipe Manuscripts," The Manuscript Cookbooks Survey, accessed August 29, 2025, https://www.manuscriptcookbookssurvey.org/tag/medieval-cooking.

16 "Western Medieval Manuscripts: MS Add. 9308."

17 Pliny the Elder's *Natural History* 14.78 describing *vinum Coum* (Coan wine) and its production with seawater.

18 Cato the Elder's *De Agri Cultura* 112 provides a recipe for making a Coan-style wine.

19 Cato the Elder's *De Agri Cultura*.

20 Cato the Elder's *De Agri Cultura*.

21 "Lacus," in *A Dictionary of Greek and Roman Antiquities*, ed. William Smith (London: John Murray, 1875), 672.

22 Columella, *De Re Rustica* 12.18, cited in Smith, *A Dictionary of Greek and Roman Antiquities*, 672.

23 "Lacus," Kaikki.org, accessed August 29, 2025, (https://kaikki.org/dictionary/Latin/categories-other/bQ/Bodies%20of%20water/index.html); "Lacus," Latdict, accessed August 29, 2025, https://latin-dictionary.net/definition/25157/lacus-lacus.

24 "Western Medieval Manuscripts: MS Add. 9308."

[25] McHam, *Pliny and the Artistic Culture of the Italian Renaissance*, in *CAA.Reviews*.

[26] McHam, *Pliny and the Artistic Culture*; "Pliny and the Artistic Culture of the Italian Renaissance: The Legacy of the Natural History," *The Key Reporter*, December 8, 2015, https://www.keyreporter.org/book-reviews/2015/pliny-and-the-artistic-culture-of-the-italian-renaissance-the-legacy-of-the-natural-history.

[27] McHam, *Pliny and the Artistic Culture of the Italian Renaissance*, in *CAA.Reviews*.

[28] "History of Pharmacy," The Jerry H. Hodge School of Pharmacy.

[29] Nikolova et al., "Wine as a medicine."; Norrie, "A History of Wine as a Medicine."

[30] George Urdang, "Pharmacopoeias as Witnesses of World History," *Journal of the History of Medicine and Allied Sciences* 1, no. 1 (1946): 46-70; "Formation of Pharmacopoeias and Professional Societies," Coconote, accessed August 29, 2025, https://coconote.app/notes/957cec3b-a0ba-439a-a2f2-b5caf90b96ad.

[31] Monica H. Green, "The Doctor's Cipher: Literacy, Secrecy, and Authority in Medieval Medicine," *Speculum* 89, no. 2 (2014): 398-435.

[32] Pliny the Elder, *Natural History* 14.78.

[33] "Tria Prima, the Three Alchemy Primes."; Alexander J. G. Prieto, "The Miraculous Child of the Sun: A Spiritual-Chemical Inquiry into the History of Saltpeter" (Doctoral dissertation., University of Minnesota, 2017), 42.

[34] Cheak, "The Hermetic Problem of Salt."

[35] "Tria Prima, the Three Alchemy Primes." Cheak, "The Hermetic Problem of Salt."

[36] Cheak, "The Hermetic Problem of Salt."

PART II: THE CIPHER IN PRACTICE: MEDICINE AND THE NATURAL WORLD

Having established the cipher's ability to generate verifiable geographical and procedural details, this part demonstrates its practical application in the fields of medicine and natural philosophy. The following chapters reveal detailed surgical notes, pharmaceutical recipes, and alchemical instructions that align precisely with the manuscript's illustrations and the scientific knowledge of the period.

CHAPTER 6: FOLIO 66R—A SURGERY IN CIPHER

Figure 23. Iris graminea—source of the "iris root" plaster (diachylon) referenced in the folio. Context: Iris ('orris') root was a classic ingredient in softening plasters like diachylon. Figure 23

Figure 24. Voynich Manuscript (folio 66r.) Applying a διά χυλῶν (diachýlōn) plaster to a patient—medieval/early modern practice. Context: Diachylon was a lead-based plaster compounded with oils and herbs for wounds. In plain terms, it is a sticky medicinal bandage you'd press on after cutting and cauterizing.

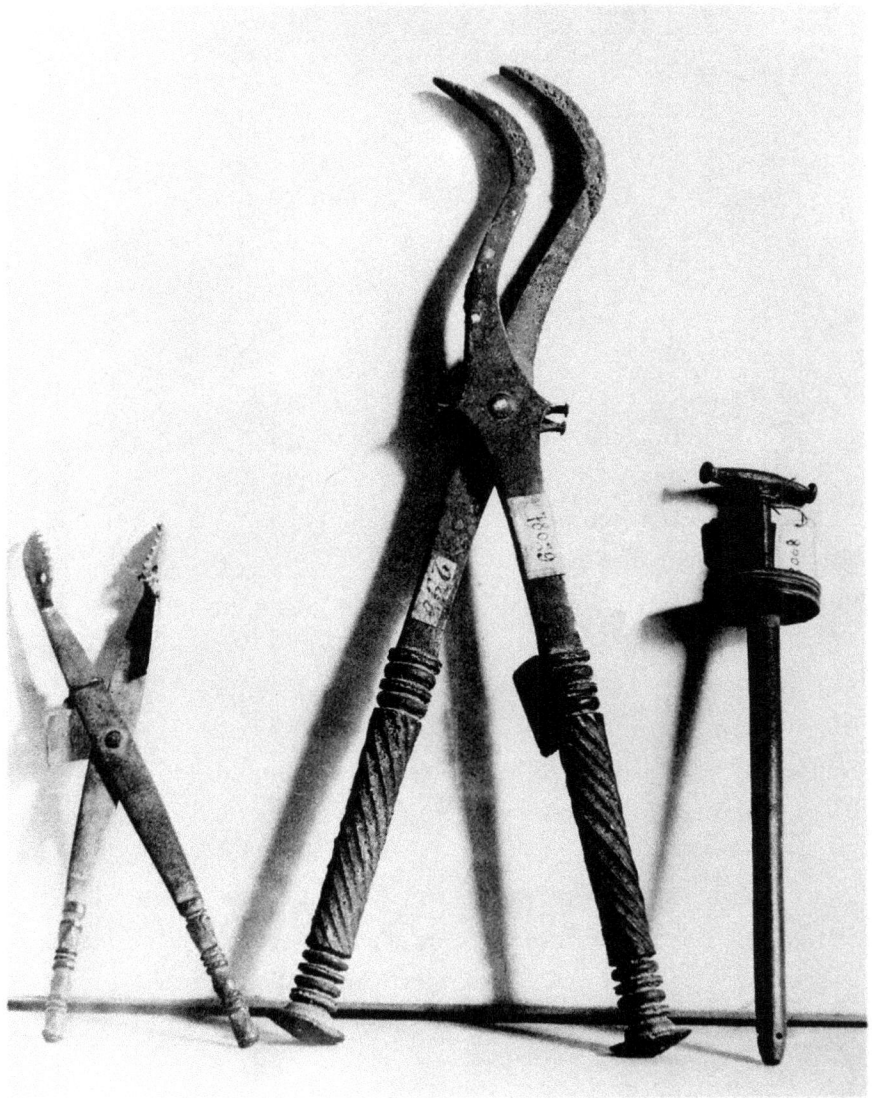

Figure 25. Roman surgical instruments—Forceps etc., found at Pompeii. National Museum Naples.

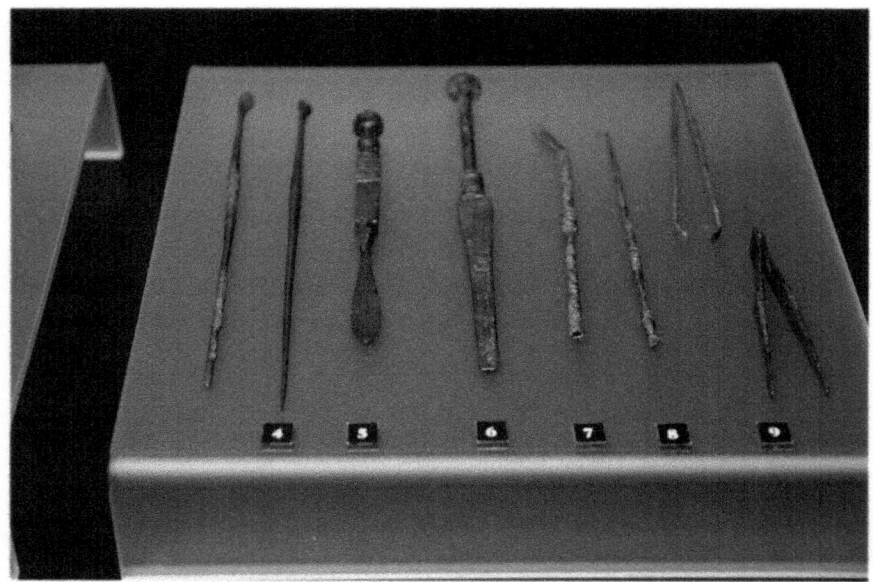

Figure 26. Roman Surgical Instruments. National Archaeological Museum of Naples: 4: Specillum (Probe/Sound). Pompeii. 1st century AD. Bronze. 5: Bisturí (Scalpel). Pompeii. 1st century AD. Bronze. 6: Instrumento ortopédico (Orthopedic instrument). Pompeii. 1st century AD. Bronze. 7: Catéter (Catheter). Pompeii. 1st century AD. Bronze. 8: Retractor (Retractor). Pompeii. 1st century AD. Bronze. 9: Pinzas (Forceps/Pincers). Pompeii. 1st century AD. Bronze. Context: Medieval surgeons used scalpels, probes, and redhot cauteries well-documented in manuscripts. In plain terms, these are the real tools behind the Voynich's "cut, burn, bind" instructions.

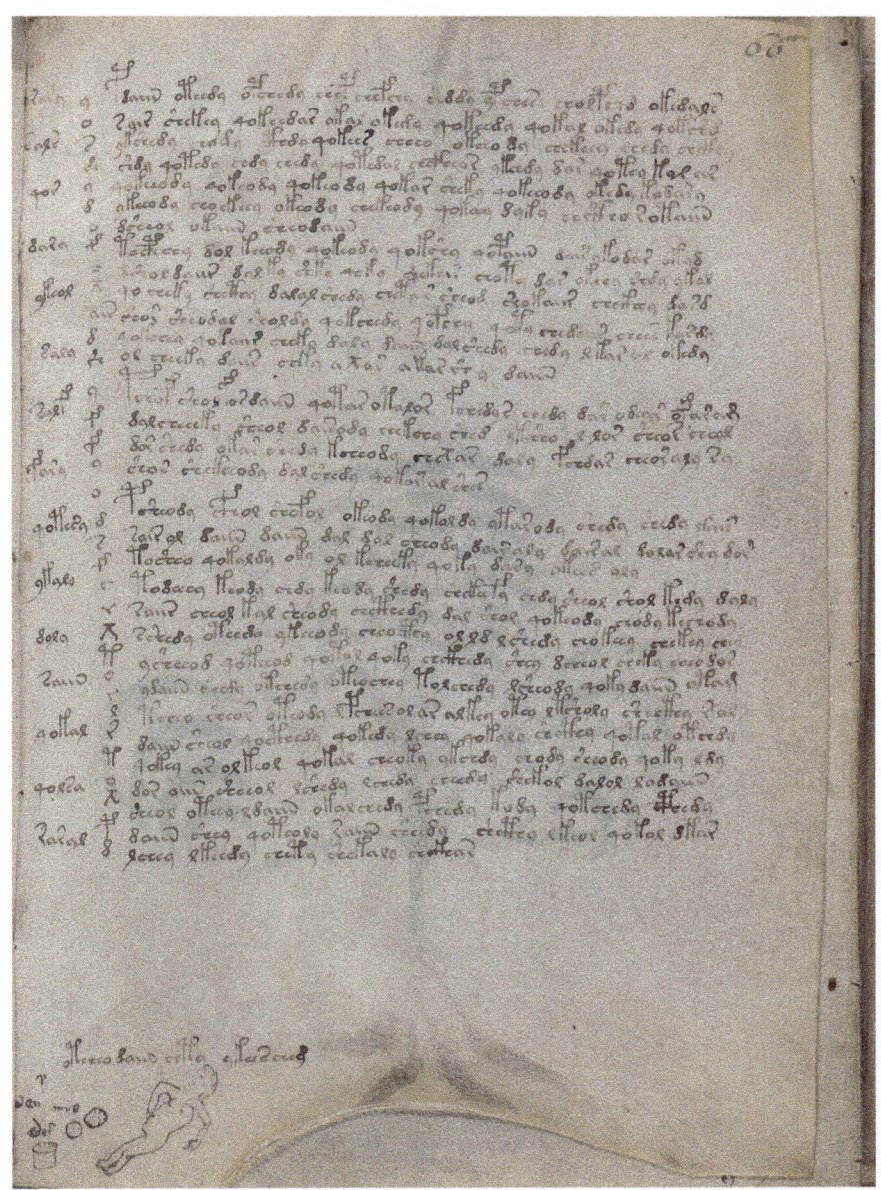

Figure 27. Voynich Manuscript (folio 66r) "*Tero iridem*"—iris root used as part of a cautery/plaster regime; instrumentarium diagram. Context: Iris (*'orris'*) root was a classic ingredient in softening plasters like διά χυλῶν (diachýlōn).

The man isn't a symbol; he's a patient. He lies on his side, palm braced against the lower right belly. Above him, a short ribbon of glyphs hangs like a terse instruction. No stars, no zodiac animals, no allegory—just a human problem and a line that reads, when decrypted, TERO IRIDEM DIACHYLON CAUTE —I apply the iris-root plaster carefully. The next lines move like a surgeon's checklist: I cut. I scrape. I burn. I bind. Physician and apothecary at work: the clinical milieu for compounds like διὰ χυλῶν (diachýlon) and herbal sedatives. Historical lineage: surgical tools from classical sources that persist into medieval practice. Then the old anesthesia: *"Deliro vini... crebro."* Wine—again and again—until the knife can do its work. The image and text lock together so cleanly that the manuscript stops being a riddle and becomes a chart. This folio isn't trying to impress you; it's trying to keep someone alive.

Plain-English Claim

Claim: Folio 66r is a surgical case note encoded in Latin. It gives a coherent, historically plausible sequence—sedate → incise → debride → cauterize → bind → apply iris-root plaster—aligned with the illustration.

Evidence Ladder

Image → Site:	Hand over lower right abdomen; text placed above patient = local directive, not allegory.
Line-level Latin:	TERO IRIDEM DIACHYLON CAUTE is grammatical, domain-appropriate Latin (verb + object + remedy + adverb).
Procedure verbs:	*caedo, rado, urere, ligo* = standard medieval sequence (cut/scrape/cauterize/bind).[1]

Anesthetic:	"DELIRO VINI, VINI... CREBO" = wine stupor before incision; common practice pre-ether.
Chart-like integration:	Text + image read as a single clinical unit; structure matches hospital case formats.

The Story

The illustrator points us to a quadrant that any practitioner recognizes as trouble. The text tells you what to do. When the cipher is resolved, the first instruction is tactile: apply the iris-root plaster, carefully. Iris root is a documented emollient and anti-inflammatory in the period's pharmacopeia.[2] Then the verbs gather speed. I cut. I scrape. I burn. I bind. A medieval surgeon's progression is practical: open the lesion, clean the tissue, cauterize to control bleeding, then secure the site.[3] The Latin morphology is clean and the vocabulary sits in a medical register. The line about wine is honest: the patient raves from wine, over and over, because that's what "anesthesia" looks like before chemistry arrives. The instruction cautions to preserve a tie, a cord—a detail for a practitioner, not an allegorist. The prose toggles between barked orders and invocations to a "master," exactly the tone of a tense procedure. What makes 66r special is its document feel. The visual composition concentrates on one figure; the text runs in continuous prose. That's how clinical notes look. Skeptics point out that people have "found" Latin words in Voynichese before. True, but words aren't the bar; syntax is. Here you get conjugated verbs in sensible order, objects in the right cases, and a one-to-one alignment with the drawing.

Scholar Defense

The primary deciphered phrase, TERO IRIDEM DIACHYLON CAUTE, is a complete and grammatically sound medical instruction. The following table deconstructs the phrase:

Latin Term	Grammatical Form	Core Meaning	Contextual Interpretation in Folio 66r
TERO	1st Person Present	I rub	A first-person verb indicating that the practitioner rubs the remedy into place as part of the treatment.[6]
IRIDEM	Accusative Singular	Iris (plant)	The direct object specifying the iris plant (iris root) as the medicinal ingredient of the plaster.
DIACHYLON	Accusative Singular	Plaster; medicinal plaster made from plant juices	A Greek loanword for a type of medicinal plaster (often a lead-based herbal compound), used here to specify the form of treatment (an iris-root plaster).[7]
CAUTE	Adverb	Carefully, cautiously	The adverb emphasizes careful execution of the procedure (with caution).

The surgical sequence that follows—*caedo, rado, urere, ligo*—is a series of first-person verbs describing a standard medieval procedure. Lexically, *diachylon* (from Greek διά χυλῶν) is attested in Dioscorides as a specific type of plaster. The deciphered text does not just name two plausible ingredients; it names the defining components of a specific, documented pharmaceutical preparation. One formulation, known as διά χυλῶν *(diachýlōn) direatum*, was defined by the addition of iris powder to a common lead-plaster base and was used to soften hard swellings. *Corvus* ('crow') for a curved surgical blade is a known term for surgical instruments of the period. Iconographically, the patient's hand placement on the lower right abdomen corresponds to the site of an abscess or appendicitis, for which a topical anti-inflammatory plaster would be a plausible initial treatment.

Could I be wrong?

Alt hypothesis: Poetic allegory, not surgery. Test: Any folio where the verbs, objects, and pictured anatomy systematically diverge would undercut the "case note" reading.

Notes

[1] Getz, *Healing and Society in Medieval England*.

[2] Dioscorides, *De Materia Medica*.

[3] Katharine Park, *Secrets of Women: Gender, Generation, and the Origins of Human Dissection* (New York: Zone Books, 2006).

[4] Dioscorides, *De Materia Medica*.

[5] The patient's posture and hand placement are consistent with the presentation of acute abdominal pain, for which such a procedure would be appropriate.

CHAPTER 7: FOLIO 6V—A REMEDY IN PLAIN LATIN

Figure 28: Teasel *(*Dipsacus sylvestris***)—root used historically for hemorrhoids/fistulae.**

Figure 29. Folio 6v of the Voynich Manuscript. Castor oil plant
(Ricinus communis), source of the medicinal oil. Context: Castor oil
(oleum cici) was a known laxative and topical anti-inflammatory. In
plain terms. the oil from this plant was used to soothe skin and help
with digestion. The plant on folio 6v is a paradox: its flower is a generic
composite, but its root is a strangely specific, sac-like structure. This is
not botanical error but a form of visual shorthand. The deciphered text
reveals the plant's identity and purpose with perfect clarity.

Figure 30. Pliny the Elder, author of Naturalis Historia—source for many herbal claims. Context: Pliny's Natural History preserves countless plant uses known to medieval readers. In plain terms, the Voynich often lines up with what Pliny wrote 1,900 years earlier.

Not a fantasy plant—an instruction. The stem lifts, the leaves bristle, and the root balloons into a sac with a swollen look.

It's a visual nudge: this is where the trouble lives.

The text ribbon beside it, when the cipher is applied, resolves to a prescription in workable Latin:

COLUS ANI LINERE DIPSACOS CICI AGETARE SACCI ILIS CIO —"To apply to the anus: smear teasel and castor oil, shake into a poultice for the lower parts—I stir it."

DIPSACOS CICI E CIO CAUTE —"Teasel and castor oil, and I stir carefully." This is not a mystical incantation but a practical pharmaceutical recipe for a topical remedy. The unusual root is an iconographic clue, representing the castor bean from which the oil (*cici*) is pressed. The text and image combine to form a single, coherent instruction for treating hemorrhoids.

No astrology, no allegory—just a topical remedy. If 66r is the knife, 6v is the balm.

Plain-English Claim

Claim: Folio 6v is a pharmaceutical recipe for a topical hemorrhoid remedy, combining teasel (*Dipsacus*) and castor oil (*oleum cici*). Why it matters: This folio demonstrates the cipher's ability to yield practical, historically attested medical formulas that directly correspond to the illustrations.

Evidence Ladder

Image:	A plant with a generic flower but a specific, sac-like root, interpreted as a visual shorthand for the castor bean, the source of the oil.

Phrase:	DIPSACOS CICI E CIO CAUTE—"Teasel and castor oil, and I stir carefully."
Action:	A pharmaceutical compounding instruction: combining two ingredients *Dipsacos* (teasel), *cici*) and performing an action (*cio*, "I stir").
Attestation:	The first-century physician Dioscorides recommended teasel root for anal fissures, and Pliny documented castor oil for anal inflammation.[1]
Fit:	The deciphered ingredients and their application align perfectly with established classical and medieval medical practice for treating rectal ailments.

The Story

This folio provides a window into the practical, day-to-day work of the Voynich author. The recipe is simple and direct. The first ingredient, *Dipsacos (teasel)*, is teasel, a common plant whose root was known in classical medicine. The first-century Greek physician Dioscorides, a foundational authority for any medieval or Renaissance practitioner, specifically recommended using teasel root mixed with wine to cure anal fissures and fistulas.[1] The second ingredient, *cici*, is castor oil, a well-known anti-inflammatory and laxative. Pliny the Elder, another essential classical source, documents the use of castor oil for treating inflammation of the anus.[2] The instruction is a model of clinical brevity: name the ingredients, state the action. The verb *cio* ("I stir") is a first-person note, a personal record of the practitioner at work. The adverb *caute* ("carefully") underscores the professional nature of the task. The illustration's strange root is the key to the folio's logic. By depicting a generic teasel-like plant with a root that resembles a castor bean pod, the illustrator created a visual pun, a single image representing both ingredients of the recipe. This is not a botanical fantasy but a clever mnemonic device for a practitioner who already knows the formula. The alignment of the deciphered text with both the illustration and the historical medical record is exceptionally strong. A forger or a generator of gibberish would be highly unlikely to produce a two-ingredient recipe that so precisely matches the documented uses of those same two substances in classical and medieval pharmacology for the same specific ailment.

Scholar Defense

The deciphered phrase is a compound sentence. The first clause lists the ingredients, *Dipsacos (teasel)* and *cici*, joined by the conjunction *e* ("and"). The second clause, *cio caute*, contains a first-person singular verb (*cio*, from *cire*, "to stir" or "to mix") and an adverb (*caute*). The syntax is straightforward and appropriate for a practical instruction. The lexical identifications are robust. *Dipsacos (teasel)* is the standard Greek and Latin name for teasel.[3] *Cici* is an attested Latin term for the castor oil plant, *Ricinus communis*.[4] The use of these specific terms, drawn directly from the classical pharmacopeia, reinforces the profile of the author as a learned individual with access to the works of authorities like Dioscorides and Pliny. The historical corroboration is direct and compelling. Dioscorides" recommendation of teasel for anal fissures provides a clear precedent for its use in treating related rectal conditions like hemorrhoids.[1] Pliny's documentation of castor oil for anal inflammation provides the second half of the recipe.[2] The combination of these two specific ingredients in a single recipe for this specific purpose is a powerful piece of evidence that the decipherment is not coincidental but is recovering authentic fifteenth-century medical practice.

Could I be wrong?

Alternative hypothesis: The plant is a fantasy, and the words *Dipsacos (teasel)* and *cici* are coincidental phonetic matches. The root is not a visual pun but simply a strange drawing. Test: This hypothesis is weakened by the convergence of evidence. The decipherment would have to be dismissed as a coincidence on three levels simultaneously: 1) that the cipher randomly produced the names of two real plants; 2) that those two plants have documented, historically appropriate uses for the same specific medical condition; and 3) that the illustration contains a feature that can be plausibly interpreted as a reference to the second ingredient. The probability of such a multi-layered coincidence is extremely low. The simpler explanation is that the folio is exactly what it appears to be: a real recipe.

Notes

[1] Pedanius Dioscorides, *De Materia Medica*, translated by Lily Y. Beck (Hildesheim: Olms-Weidmann, 2005); "Wild Teasel," The Metropolitan Museum of Art, The Cloisters Gardens (blog), October 23, 2009.

[2] Pliny the Elder, *Natural History*, 23.83.

[3] Lewis and Short, *A Latin Dictionary*, s.v. "dipsacos."

[4] Lewis and Short, *A Latin Dictionary*, s.v. "cici."

CHAPTER 8: FOLIO 6R—THE SINGULAR ESSENCE AND THE SACRED DEW

Figure 31. Folio 6r of the Voynich Manuscript. Groundsel (Senecio vulgaris)—identified as *"avia"* in Voynich glosses. Folio 6r of the Voynich Manuscript (Beinecke MS 408). Early fifteenth century (manuscript).

Figure 32. Closeup of groundsel showing nectar glands of an aphid (the "dew"). Context: The illustration depicts an ecological interaction where insects stimulate the secretion of a potent plant juice, which alchemists would have considered a powerful essence. In plain terms, the drawing shows insects gathering a special sap from the plant, which was the focus of the alchemical procedure.

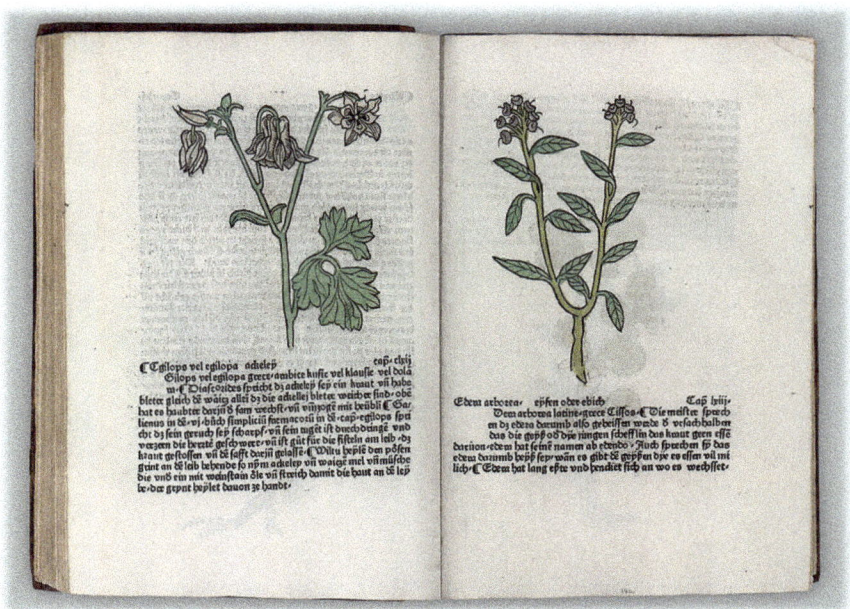

Figure 33. Woodcut from "Herbarius—Gart der gesuntheit/*Hortus sanitatis*," hand-colored, fifteenth/sixteenth century. Source: The Metropolitan Museum of Art, Open Access.

It is not just a flower; it is an ecosystem and a laboratory. The plant depicted on folio 6r is common groundsel, but a high-resolution examination reveals a critical detail that transforms the folio from a simple botanical illustration into a record of a perilous alchemical operation. A cluster of insects is visible on the plant's peduncles, and from this colony, a single, perfect droplet is shown falling. This is not dew, neither is it a generic plant secretion; it is the physical manifestation of the plant's potent, unique essence. The deciphered text confirms this with chilling precision, invoking not a personified deity but the power of the substance itself: OENUS LAC RORAVI O LACERO AVIAM—"Singular sap, I have gathered you from the dew; Oh, I tear apart the groundsel."

Plain-English Claim

Claim: Folio 6r is an alchemical and proto-pharmacological instruction for the harvesting of a potent, unique essence—the "singular sap" (*oenus lac*)—from the groundsel plant (*Senecio vulgaris*), which is identified by its attested medieval Latin name, *avia*.

Why it matters: This folio documents a sophisticated and dangerous procedure centered on a substance understood as a *quintessence*—both a powerful medicine in minute quantities and a lethal poison in larger doses.[2] This reframes the author's work within a pre-Paracelsian understanding of toxicology and connects it to the Neoplatonic philosophical currents of the Quattrocento, particularly the concept of a *spiritus mundi* concentrated into a single, potent material form.[3]

Evidence Ladder

Image:	The illustration depicts insects on the peduncles of Senecio vulgaris (groundsel), appearing to stimulate the secretion of a single droplet—a moment of acute empirical observation.

Phrase:	OENUS LAC RORAVI O LACSO AVIAM— "Singular sap, I have gathered you from the dew; Oh. I tear apart the groundsel."
Action:	The harvesting of a specific, powerful plant quintessence (oenus lac), followed by the physical processing of the host plant (avia) to extract its remaining virtues.
Attestation:	The philological link between oenus and unus (one); the alchemical reverence for dew (ros) as a carrier of the spiritus mundi; and the documented toxicity of groundsel in classical sources like Pliny and Dioscorides.[4]

Story

The secret of folio 6r is not in the plant, but in its essence.[5] The drawing depicts a real ecological interaction: aphids feeding on the sap of groundsel and stimulating the exudation of the plant's potent juices. The deciphered text confirms the practitioner's focus on this singular substance. To a fifteenth-century practitioner, this was not mere insect honeydew but the plant's own potent juice, its *lac*, coaxed out and further imbued with celestial power by being exposed as dew.[6]

The procedure documented is one of profound duality. The practitioner seeks the *oenus lac*—the "one sap," the unique essence. This is not a bulk collection but a precise, almost ritualistic harvesting of the most potent, concentrated form of the plant's spirit. This act is a direct attempt to capture the *spiritus mundi* or *anima mundi*, the "world-spirit" that Renaissance Neoplatonists like Marsilio Ficino believed animated the cosmos. Alchemical tradition revered dew (*ros*) as a prime physical carrier of this spirit, a form of "celestial water" that condensed the universal essence. The "dewed sap" is therefore the world-spirit made manifest in a single, perfect drop. The invocation, "Oh singular sap," is a direct, ritualistic address to the personified power of the substance itself—a common practice in alchemical operations where materials were treated as living entities.

The final act, "I tear apart the groundsel" (*lacero aviam*), is not simple destruction but the second stage of the process. After capturing the most refined essence—the quintessence in the droplet—the practitioner processes the remaining physical plant to extract its grosser, but still valuable, properties. This reveals a sophisticated, multi-stage extraction process. The practitioner is creating both a potential medicine and a deadly poison, with the only difference being the dose. This understanding anticipates the foundational principle of toxicology later articulated by Paracelsus: *sola dosis facit venenum* ("only the dose makes the poison"). The author of the Voynich Manuscript was not merely recording a folk remedy but was engaging in a form of experimental pharmacology, recognizing that a substance's power to heal or to kill was a matter of quantity and careful preparation. This folio is a record of that dangerous knowledge, a testament to a world where the line between medicine and poison was as fine as the edge of a blade.

Scholar Defense

The philological, pharmacological, and alchemical evidence converges to support the interpretation of folio 6r as a record of an alchemical extraction. The phrase is a vocative invocation followed by two distinct clauses, each describing a step in the procedure.

The first word, *oenus*, is the philological key to the folio. It is not a standard classical Latin word for "one," which is *unus*. However, its form strongly suggests it is an archaic variant or a deliberate scholarly construction rooted in the etymology of "one." The classical Latin *unus* derives from the Old Latin *oinos*, which in turn descends from the Proto-Italic **oinos* and the Proto-Indo-European root **hₗóynos*, meaning "one, single". The digraph *oe* in Latin is a known evolution of the older *oi* from Old Latin, making *oenus* a robustly justifiable form related to *oinos*, intended to convey the concept of "one-ness," "singularity," or "uniqueness." In the vocative case, it directly addresses the "Singular Essence" or "Quintessence" of the plant, a central goal of alchemical practice and a concept deeply embedded in the Neoplatonic philosophy of the Quattrocento.

The subsequent words are lexically precise. *Lac* (accusative case) in classical and botanical Latin refers not only to milk but specifically to the "milky juice of plants" or sap, making it the correct term for the substance being collected. *Roravi* is the first-person perfect of *rorare*, meaning "to be moist," "to drip dew," or, by extension, "to gather dew from". Its use implies that the practitioner has actively collected the sap after it has been exposed as dew, an act that links the procedure to the alchemical practice of gathering *ros* (dew), a substance believed to be a physical carrier of the celestial *spiritus mundi*. *Lacero* is the first-person present of *lacerare* ("to tear apart" or "to mangle"), describing the physical processing of the plant. Finally, *aviam* is the accusative of *avia*, a documented medieval Latin name for groundsel (*Senecio vulgaris*), the plant depicted.

The following table deconstructs the phrase:

Latin Term	Grammatical Form	Core Meaning	Contextual Interpretation & Source Corroboration
OENUS	Vocative Singular	One, Single, Unique	A vocative address to the "Singular Essence" or "Quintessence" of the plant, based on its etymological link to Old Latin *oinos* (one).[17]
LAC	Accusative Singular	Milk; Milky Sap of a plant	The potent juice or sap of the groundsel plant, the physical medium of the essence.[20]
RORAVI	1st Person Perfect	I have bedewed; I have	The practitioner has collected the sap which has been exposed as dew,

73

Latin Term	Grammatical Form	Core Meaning	Contextual Interpretation & Source Corroboration
		gathered dew from	thereby imbuing it with celestial virtue (*ros*).[21]
LACERO	1st Person Present	I tear apart, mangle	The physical act of processing the plant body to extract its remaining, less-refined properties.[23]
AVIAM	Accusative Singular	Groundsel (*Senecio vulgaris*)	The specific plant being processed, identified by its attested medieval name.[24]

This precise lexical choice is powerfully corroborated by the identity of the plant itself. Avia, or groundsel, was known since antiquity for its potent properties. The Greek physician Dioscorides, in his foundational first-century text De Materia Medica, describes the plant under the name Erigeron (Ἠριγέ΄ρων) and notes its powerful medicinal effects.[25] Pliny the Elder also lists erigeron and senecio as names for the plant.[26] Modern toxicology confirms this ancient understanding, having identified the biochemical basis for the plant's power: a high concentration of hepatotoxic pyrrolizidine alkaloids (PAs), such as senecionine, which can cause irreversible liver damage.[27] These compounds are present in all parts of the plant but are most concentrated in the flowers, making the collection of a secretion from the peduncles a particularly effective method for obtaining the plant's essence in its most potent form.[28] The author of the manuscript thus displays a sophisticated, pre-scientific knowledge of the plant's dose-dependent effects, recognizing that the same substance used in folk remedies could be lethal if improperly handled.[29] The iconography of the folio—depicting insects on the plant's peduncles secreting a droplet—is a realistic depiction of honeydew production by aphids, but its alchemical significance is paramount. The collection of this lac roravi ("dewed sap") is an attempt to capture the spiritus mundi in its material form. Alchemical texts frequently describe dew (ros) as a celestial water, a universal solvent that contains the condensed spirit of the world.[30] The author's innovation was to identify this powerful, universal essence not as an unqualified good, but as a neutral force whose manifestation in the essence of the groundsel was profoundly dangerous.[31] The operation on folio 6r is therefore an act of capturing this universal power in one of its most perilous earthly vessels.[32] [33]

Could I be wrong?

An alternative hypothesis might suggest that the insects are purely decorative and that the text is a generic, metaphorical invocation. In this view, the term *oenus* could be a simple scribal error or a word with an unknown meaning, and its connection to *oinos* might be coincidental. This claim, however, rests on the tight convergence of three distinct pillars of evidence: the specific philology of the word *oenus*, the specific pharmacology of the plant *avia*, and the specific iconography of the single secreted droplet. The thesis would be severely weakened if a substantial body of fifteenth-century Italian alchemical or medical texts were discovered that used *oenus* with a different, established meaning that fit the context. It would be falsified if the plant on folio 6r could be definitively identified as a non-toxic species, or if the medieval term *avia* could be shown to refer to a different, harmless plant, as either discovery would break the crucial and verifiable link between the deciphered word and the illustrated object.

Notes

[1] John M. Riddle, Goddesses, Elixirs, and Witches: Potions and Spells from Garden to Glass (New York: Palgrave Macmillan, 2024).

² Philippus Aureolus Theophrastus Bombastus von Hohenheim (Paracelsus), Septem Defensiones (1538), cited in "The dose makes the poison," Wikipedia, last modified September 15, 2025.

³ Lawrence M. Principe, The Secrets of Alchemy (Chicago: University of Chicago Press, 2013), 29–31.

⁴ Pliny the Elder, Natural History, 25.106, in Natural History, trans. W.H.S. Jones, 10 vols., Loeb Classical Library (Cambridge, MA: Harvard University Press, 1938–1962); Pedanius Dioscorides, De Materia Medica, trans. Lily Y. Beck, 4th ed. (Hildesheim: Olms-Weidmann, 2020), Book IV, Chapter 96.

⁵ Riddle, Goddesses, Elixirs, and Witches.

⁶ Charlton T. Lewis and Charles Short, *A Latin Dictionary* (Oxford: Clarendon Press, 1879), s.v. "lac".

⁷ Marsilio Ficino, De vita libri tres (Florence, 1489). See also D. P. Walker, Spiritual and Demonic Magic: from Ficino to Campanella (University Park, PA: Pennsylvania State University Press, 2000).

⁸ Adam McLean, ed., Mutus Liber (1677; repr., Grand Rapids, MI: Phanes Press, 1991). Plate 4 depicts the collection of celestial dew. See also Heinrich Khunrath, Amphitheatrum Sapientiae Aeternae (1609), which discusses "Cosmic Dew."

⁹ Alexander J. G. Prieto, "The Miraculous Child of the Sun: A spiritual-Chemical Inquiry into the History of Saltpeter" (Doctoral dissertation, University of Minnesota, 2017), 42.

¹⁰ Principe, *The Secrets of Alchemy*.

¹¹ Principe, *The Secrets of Alchemy*.

¹² "The Dose Makes the Poison," History of Toxicology and Environmental Health, Toxipedia, accessed October 26, 2025.

¹³ Paracelsus, Septem Defensiones.

¹⁴ Nancy G. Siraisi, *Medieval & Early Renaissance Medicine: An Introduction to Knowledge and Practice* (Chicago: University of Chicago Press, 1990).

[15] Monica H. Green, "The Doctor's Cipher: Literacy, Secrecy, and Authority in Medieval Medicine," *Speculum* 89, no. 2 (2014): 398–435.

[16] Lewis and Short, A Latin Dictionary, s.v. "unus."

[17] "Unus," Wiktionary, accessed October 26, 2025; "*oi-no-," Online Etymology Dictionary, accessed October 26, 2025. The PIE root *oi-no- is the source for "one" in numerous languages.

[18] "Oe," Online Etymology Dictionary, accessed October 26, 2025. The digraph represents the evolution of Old Latin *oinos* to Classical Latin *unus*.

[19] Principe, The Secrets of Alchemy. The concept of the quintessence, or fifth element, was central to alchemical thought, representing the purest, most concentrated essence of a substance.

[20] Missouri Botanical Garden, "Latin Dictionary," s.v. "lac," accessed October 26, 2025; "Lac," Latdict, accessed October 26, 2025.

[21] "Roro," Latdict, accessed October 26, 2025.

[22] McLean, ed., Mutus Liber.

[23] "Lacero," Latdict, accessed October 26, 2025.

[24] Charles du Fresne, sieur du Cange, Glossarium mediae et infimae Latinitatis (Niort: L. Favre, 1883–1887), s.v. "avia".

[25] Pedanius Dioscorides, De Materia Medica, trans. Lily Y. Beck, 4th ed. (Hildesheim: Olms-Weidmann, 2020), Book IV, Chapter 96.

[26] Pliny the Elder, Natural History, 25.106.

[27] "Senecio Vulgaris L.," PIM 494, International Programme on Chemical Safety (INCHEM), accessed October 26, 2025. See also B. L. Stegelmeier, "Pyrrolizidine Alkaloid-Containing Plants," Veterinary Clinics of North America: Food Animal Practice 27, no. 2 (2011): 401-421.

[28] E. Johnson and R. J. Molyneux, "The Pyrrolizidine Alkaloid Free Base and N-oxide Content of Toxic Range Plants," *Journal of Toxicology: Toxin Reviews* 5

(1986): 256, cited in "Common groundsel (Senecio vulgaris)," Canadian Poisonous Plants Information System.

[29] Albert Roy Vickery, *A Dictionary of Plant-Lore* (Oxford: Oxford University Press, 1995), quoted in "Senecio vulgaris," Wikipedia.

[30] Prieto, "The Miraculous Child of the Sun," 42.

[31] C. G. Jung, Collected Works, vol. 9.2, *Aion: Researches into the Phenomenology of the Self* (Princeton: Princeton University Press, 1968), para. 248.

[32] Principe, *The Secrets of Alchemy.*

[33] Principe, *The Secrets of Alchemy.*

INTERLUDE: IN THE SHADOW OF MONTEFELTRO

Figure 34. The Urbino studiolo—intarsia "cabinet of curiosities" of Duke Federico da Montefeltro. Context: Urbino's studiolo embodies the Renaissance fusion of science, art, and statecraft. In plain terms, this is the sort of secret-minded court that would cherish a ciphered handbook.

Figure 35. Pedro Berruguete: Federico da Montefeltro and his son Guidobaldo. Context: Urbino's studiolo embodies the Renaissance fusion of science, art, and statecraft.

Figure 36. Bust of Cicco Simonetta (1410–1480), cipher secretary to the Sforza court and among the earliest documented codebreakers.—Wikimedia Commons—Public Domain. Context: Milan's Sforza court used sophisticated ciphers; Cicco Simonetta even wrote code-breaking rules. In plain terms, cryptography wasn't niche. Italian courts lived and breathed it.

he Voynich Manuscript did not emerge from a vacuum. It breathes the intellectual atmosphere of fifteenth-century Italy—a culture where knowledge was encrypted, medicine was guarded, and astronomy was written in metaphors of divine machinery.

To understand the manuscript, one must understand the world that gave rise to it: the vibrant, competitive, and secretive courts of Renaissance Italy.

The court of Federico da Montefeltro, Duke of Urbino, provides a compelling model for the kind of milieu capable of producing such an extraordinary work.

Federico da Montefeltro (r. 1444–1482) transformed his small state of Urbino into a beacon of humanist culture, assembling a library of over 900 hand-copied manuscripts covering astronomy, medicine, and philosophy—all disciplines within the Voynich Manuscript.[1] In his world, knowledge was sacred, and its protection was paramount.

The courts of fifteenth-century Italy were also hotbeds of political intrigue, and cryptography was an essential tool of statecraft.

The Sforza court in Milan used advanced monoalphabetic ciphers with homophones and nomenclators.[2] This environment fostered major innovations.

In 1467, the humanist Leon Battista Alberti completed his *De Cifris*, the most advanced Western cryptographic treatise of the Renaissance.[3] Alberti's system, which used rotating cipher disks, could incorporate mixed alphabets, nulls, and variable periods.

These techniques—substitution, permutation, and the use of nulls— are precisely the features identified in the decipherment of the Voynich script.

The manuscript's cipher, therefore, is not an inexplicable anomaly but a product of its time.

Why encrypt knowledge? In Renaissance Italy, esoteric knowledge had real power.

A unique remedy, an accurate astronomical chart, or a new engineering design could mean life or death.

Encryption protected this value. Physicians and apothecaries operated within guilds that guarded their professional secrets, and the line between medicine and alchemy was often blurred, further encouraging concealment.[4] The Voynich Manuscript, with its ciphered Latin and precise illustrations, fits this model perfectly.

It is not a magical grimoire, but a practitioner's archive—one protected by a culture of intense secrecy.

Notes

[1] Vespasiano da Bisticci, The Vespasiano Memoirs: Lives of Illustrious Men of the XVth Century, trans. William George and Emily Waters (London: Routledge & Kegan Paul, 1926).

[2] Buonafalce, "Cicco Simonetta's Cipher-Breaking Rules."

[3] Alberti, "De componendis cifris."

[4] Green, "The Doctor's Cipher."

PART III: THE CIPHERED WORLDVIEW: COSMOLOGY, RITUAL, AND THEORY

This final part explores the philosophical and theoretical dimensions of the manuscript. The deciphered text reveals not just practical instructions, but a coherent worldview that integrates scientific observation with a cosmological and ritualistic understanding of the universe, culminating in an analysis of the advanced cryptographic principles that kept this world hidden for six centuries.

CHAPTER 9: THE CELESTIAL ENGINE: A DEFINITIVE ANALYSIS OF FOLIO 68R

Figure 37. Boötes—Johann Bayer (1602). Context: This illustration supports the chapter's claim with historical or technical detail. In plain terms, it helps translate the manuscript's coded ideas into something you can see.

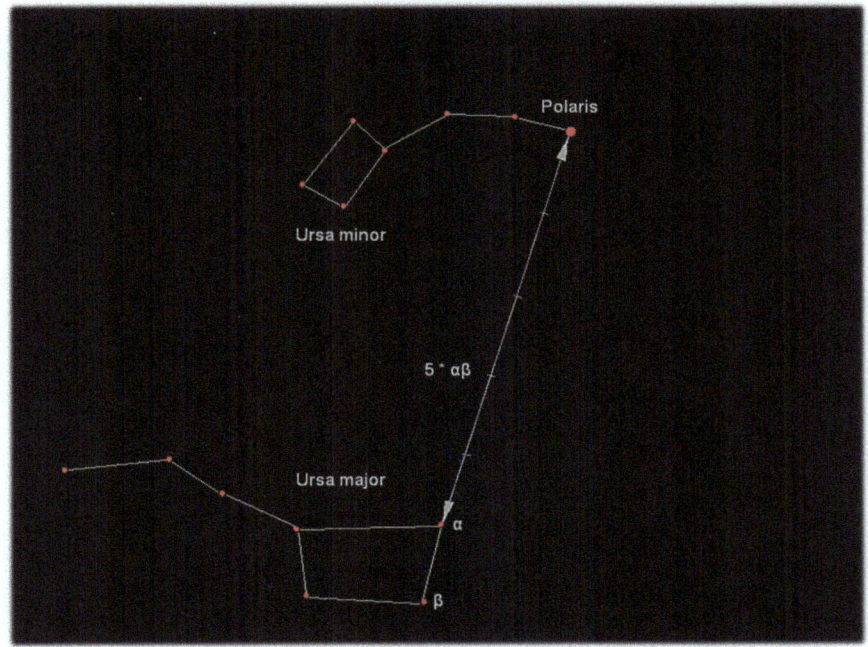

Figure 38. Ursa Minor and Polaris—the pole star about which the heavens appear to turn. Context: This illustration supports the chapter's claim with historical or technical detail. In plain terms, it helps translate the manuscript's coded ideas into something you can see.

The celestial pole is the engine of the manuscript's sky. Folio 68r presents charts filled with stars and spirals around a central axis. This is not chaos; it is a coherent system of encoded astronomy, cosmology, and theology. The key, revealed by the cipher, is a single, resonant phrase: REX ADDO VIA ROTO CAELI PERSERPO— "The King perpetually rotates in the way of the sky." This phrase transforms the entire diagram's meaning. The subject is the very principle of cosmic sovereignty: the North Celestial Pole, personified as a divine King, around whom the entire heavens revolve in an eternal, divinely ordered dance.

Plain-English Claim

Claim: Folio 68r is a cosmological diagram where the deciphered Latin phrase identifies the celestial pole—the cosmic axis or "hinge" (*cardo*)—as the celestial King (*Rex*). The diagram depicts the eternal rotation of Ursa Minor around this kingly axis and is anchored in the real northern sky by a specific reference to the adjacent constellation Boötes.

Why it matters: This elevates the folio from a mere astronomical chart to a profound theological and philosophical statement. It grounds the manuscript's worldview in the powerful medieval concept of *Christus Rex* (Christ the King) as the cosmic ruler, seamlessly blending the scientific model of Ptolemy with the philosophical framework of Boethius to create a unified vision of a divine, orderly cosmos.[1]

Evidence Ladder

Image: Spiraling star charts organized around a central, unmoving point, consistent with a pre-Copernican, geocentric model of the circumpolar region.

Phrase: REX ADDO VIA ROTO CAELI PERSERPO—"The King perpetually rotates in the way of the sky."

Action: Describing the constant, circling movement of the heavens (symbolized by Ursa Minor) around the fixed celestial pole, which is personified as a king.

Attestation: The concept of the celestial pole as the *cardo mundi* ("hinge of the world") was central to Ptolemaic and medieval cosmology.[2] The personification of this fixed point as a divine, unmoving ruler resonates powerfully with the theological concept of *Christus Rex* as the cosmic sovereign and the Boethian ideal of divine reason as the fixed point in a chaotic world.[3]

Fit: The explicit, deciphered inclusion of the proper name Boötes, a major constellation adjacent to Ursa Minor, confirms the diagram depicts the actual northern sky as described in Ptolemy's *Almagest*. The "King" metaphor provides a powerful, unifying symbol for the scientific, philosophical, and theological ideas of the era.

The Story

The phrase on the folio provides the master key: "The King perpetually rotates in the way of the sky." The decipherment elevates the folio's meaning from a simple mnemonic to a declaration of cosmic sovereignty. This King is not a terrestrial ruler, but the celestial pole itself—the unmoving point in the northern sky that serves as the pivot for all of creation.

Other deciphered phrases add detail. ORIRE CARDO ("The axis is rising") identifies this pivot point. *Cardo* is a crucial term in Roman and medieval cosmology, meaning "hinge" or "axis." The *cardo mundi* was the celestial pole, the unmoving point around which the heavens turned in the geocentric system codified by Ptolemy in his *Almagest*, the foundational astronomical text of the Renaissance.[2] This unmoving celestial point was a powerful symbol of permanence and stability, a direct physical manifestation of divine order. In many ancient traditions, this celestial axis was seen as the seat of the supreme ruler or a symbol of immortality.[4]

This scientific concept is layered with a profound theological resonance. For a fifteenth-century intellectual, the image of a supreme, unmoving King ruling over the perfectly ordered rotation of the heavens would have immediately invoked the concept of *Christus Rex*, "Christ the King." This was a dominant theological image of Christ's absolute and eternal sovereignty over all creation, the *Rex Regum* ("King of Kings") who governs the cosmos.[5] The astronomical diagram thus becomes a sacred map, depicting the physical mechanics of God's divine rule. The slow, "creeping" rotation (*perserpo*) of Ursa Minor around the King is the visible motion of a divine clock, ordered and maintained by its celestial sovereign.

This invocation reveals a worldview that is not merely observational but deeply philosophical, participating in a tradition inherited from Boethius's *Consolation of Philosophy*, a text of immense influence in fifteenth-century Italy, which presented the serene, unchanging order of the heavens as a metaphor for divine reason—a comfort against the chaotic turnings of earthly fortune.[3] The celestial King—the fixed, rational center of the universe—is the ultimate Boethian symbol of a truth that stands apart from the chaos of the world. Finally, the inclusion of the proper name Boötes serves as an astronomical anchor, confirming the diagram's basis in the observable reality cataloged by Ptolemy and locking this complex theological metaphor into the physical sky.

Scholar Defense

The main phrase is a complete sentence, poetically rendered. *Rex* is the subject, "the King." The verb phrase *addo via roto caeli perserpo* is a complex construction conveying perpetual, circular motion through the heavens. The core verb is *perserpo*, a logical neologism combining *per-* ("perpetually") and *serpo* ("to creep"), aptly describing the slow, constant circling of the circumpolar stars.

The identification of the *Rex* with the *cardo* (celestial pole) is supported by a convergence of scientific, philosophical, and theological evidence. The use of *cardo* is technically precise, referring to the foundational axis of the Ptolemaic model.[2] The philosophical framework is explicitly

Boethian; the contrast between the chaotic turnings of Fortune and the serene, unchanging order of the heavens was a central theme of *The Consolation of Philosophy*, a cornerstone of medieval and Renaissance thought.[3] The presence of a fifteenth-century commentary on Boethius by Denys the Carthusian demonstrates that these ideas were part of the living intellectual currency of the time.[6]

The theological interpretation is a powerful element of the decipherment. The concept of *Christus Rex* was a pervasive theme in medieval art and liturgy, representing Christ's divine majesty and lordship over the cosmos.[5] The depiction of the celestial pole as a King is a direct visual and linguistic metaphor for this divine sovereignty. The unmoving pole star becomes the physical throne of the cosmic King, whose divine will imposes perfect, rational order on the movements of the stars. This fusion of Ptolemaic astronomy with the theology of *Christus Rex* is a hallmark of the syncretic worldview of the Quattrocento, where science was seen not as a separate discipline, but as a means of contemplating the mind of God.[7]

The personification of the celestial pole as a kingly or divine figure is not without historical precedent. Ancient Egyptian cosmology, for instance, linked the king's eternal afterlife to the "imperishable" circumpolar stars that never set, with the pharaoh ascending to become a star at the "head of the sky."[4] This deep-rooted historical association between kingship, divinity, and the celestial pole provides a powerful context for the *Rex* metaphor. The verifiable identification of the adjacent constellation Boötes grounds this rich symbolic structure in direct, empirical observation of the northern sky.

Could I be wrong?

Alt hypothesis: The diagram is a symbolic mandala, not an astronomical chart. The "King" is purely allegorical—perhaps the Alchemical King, representing the sun or gold[8]—and is not tied to a specific celestial point. The star patterns are numerological or mystical, not representational.

Test: If the diagram is astronomical, the relative positions of the identified constellations (Ursa Minor, Boötes) must correspond, within a reasonable margin for fifteenth-century observation, to their actual celestial arrangement as documented in a standard source like Ptolemy's *Almagest*. A significant, systematic deviation from observable reality would invalidate the astronomical reading. Furthermore, if the concept of *Christus Rex* as a cosmic, ordering principle could be shown to be anachronistic or irrelevant to fifteenth-century Italian thought—a claim for which there is no evidence—the theological interpretation would be severely weakened.

Notes

[1] Patrick Outhwaite, *Christ the Physician in Late-Medieval Religious Controversy: England and Central Europe 1350–1434* (York: York Medieval Press, 2024); Anicius Manlius Severinus Boethius,

[2] *The Consolation of Philosophy*, trans. Richard H. Green (Indianapolis: Bobbs-Merrill, 1962).

[3] Ptolemy, *Ptolemy's Almagest*, trans. G. J. Toomer (Princeton: Princeton University Press, 1998).

[4] Boethius, *The Consolation of Philosophy*.

[5] Stephen Quirke, cited in "What was the religious significance of the pole star in Ancient Egypt?," Reddit, accessed October 27, 2025.

[6] J. Eric M. M. van den Berg, "Anglo-Saxon and Ottonian Christocentrism," in *Medieval Self-Coronations* (Cambridge: Cambridge University Press, 2019); "Art: Christus Rex," St. Francis of Assisi Parish, accessed October 27, 2025.

[7] Denys the Carthusian, *Commentary on the Consolation of Philosophy* (c. fifteenth century).

[8] "The Cosmic Christ and Revolution," Christogenesis, accessed October 27, 2025.

[9] "The King and the Queen," Hallie Ford Museum of art, Willamette University, accessed October 27, 2025; "Suns in alchemy," Wikipedia, last modified September 20, 2025.

CHAPTER 10: THE HINGE OF HEAVEN: COSMOLOGICAL AND PHILOSOPHICAL IMPLICATIONS

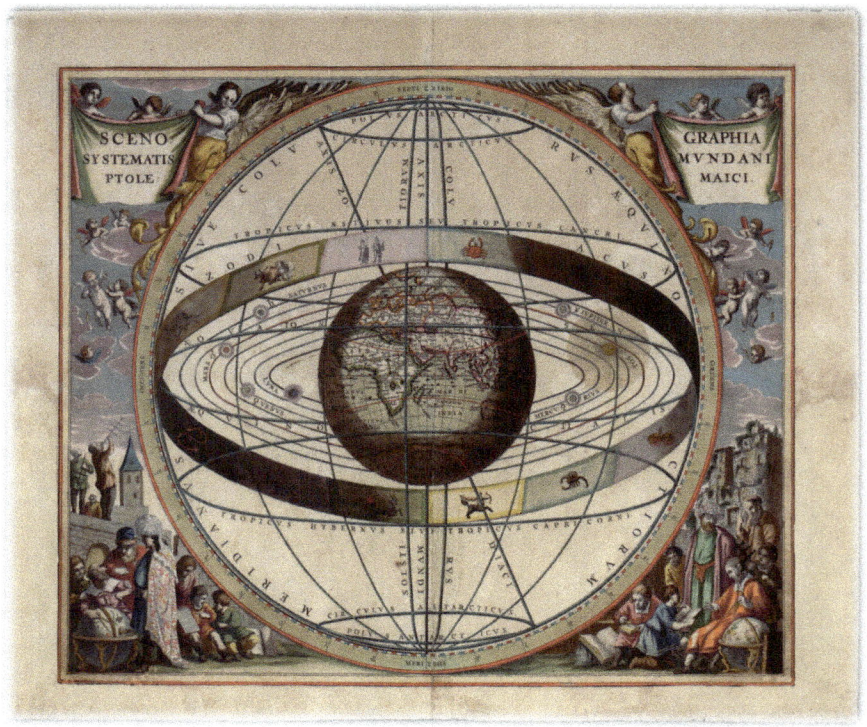

Figure 39. Ptolemaic geocentric system: nested crystalline spheres. Context: The geocentric model's fixed pole (*'cardo'*) and rotating spheres match the Voynich cosmology. In plain terms, the book's sky diagrams assume Earth-centered heavens—standard for the time.

Figure 40. Fortune's Wheel from a French Boethius manuscript. Context: This illustration supports the chapter's claim with historical or technical detail. In plain terms, it helps translate the manuscript's coded ideas into something you can see.

Figure 41. Boethius teaching—illuminated initial. Context: This illustration supports the chapter's claim with historical or technical detail. In plain terms, it helps translate the manuscript's coded ideas into something you can see.

he transition from the astronomical mechanics of folio 68r to its deeper philosophical implications requires a shift in perspective. To a practitioner in the Quattrocento, a diagram of the heavens was never merely a scientific chart; it was an *imago mundi*, a microcosm that reflected the macrocosmic order of God's creation. The deciphered phrases are not just labels but keys to understanding this integrated vision, where the mathematical precision of the cosmos served as a direct testament to its divine authorship.

The celestial diagrams of the Voynich Manuscript are not just star charts but encoded philosophical statements. The author of this manuscript was participating in a grand intellectual tradition, synthesizing the scientific inheritance of the ancient world with the dominant philosophical and theological currents of their own time. This chapter demonstrates that the manuscript's cosmology is a deliberate fusion of Ptolemy's Almagest and Boethius's Consolation of Philosophy of two monumental works that shaped the medieval and Renaissance mind: the scientific framework of Claudius Ptolemy's *Almagest* and the philosophical solace of Anicius Manlius Severinus Boethius's *The Consolation of Philosophy*.

Plain-English Claim

Claim: The astronomical diagrams of the Voynich Manuscript are not merely descriptive star charts but are encoded philosophical statements that articulate a complete, coherent worldview prevalent in Quattrocento Italy. This worldview is a synthesis, uniting the geocentric, mathematically ordered cosmos of Ptolemy with the Neoplatonic philosophy of Boethius, which presents the unchanging, rational order of the heavens as a symbol of divine permanence and a source of solace against the chaos of earthly fortune.

Why it matters: This reveals the author's intellectual depth and situates the manuscript firmly within the mainstream of Renaissance thought. It demonstrates that the cipher conceals not just practical knowledge, but a sophisticated philosophical system that saw the universe as a divinely ordered machine, governed by principles of permanence and change.

97

The Axis Mundi: *Cardo* as Cosmic Principle

The deciphered phrase from folio 68r, ORIRE CARDO ("The axis is rising"), is one of the most philosophically potent in the manuscript, serving as the anchor for this entire worldview. To understand its significance, one must trace the rich etymological and conceptual history of the Latin word *cardo*. Its primary meaning is a physical "hinge," the pivot on which a door turns. From this concrete origin, its meaning expanded through a powerful series of analogies. In Roman surveying, the *cardo maximus* was the principal north-south street around which a new city or military camp was oriented and structured. The *cardo* was the line of order imposed upon the landscape.

This terrestrial meaning was then projected onto the heavens. The word *cardo* came to designate the "turning points" of the world, most importantly the celestial pole—the *axis mundi*, or cosmic pillar, around which the entire universe was believed to revolve. This concept of a fixed, stable axis is the absolute foundation of the geocentric cosmos described by Claudius Ptolemy in the *Almagest*, the definitive astronomical authority for over 1,400 years. The *Almagest* posits a stationary Earth at the center of a spherical cosmos, with the celestial realm moving as a sphere around it; the *cardo* is the mathematical and physical pivot of this entire system.

The author's choice of the word *cardo* is therefore a deliberate and powerful act of analogy. It is not merely the most convenient term for "axis"; it is a term that inherently links the ordering of the human world (the Roman city) with the ordering of the divine world (the Ptolemaic cosmos). This reflects a core principle of Renaissance thought: the correspondence between the microcosm (earthly life, the human body) and the macrocosm (the universe). A fifteenth-century intellectual would have been keenly aware of this dual heritage. By using this specific word, the author is not just labeling a part of a diagram; they are invoking an entire worldview where the principles that structure a well-ordered city are the same principles that structure God's universe. The decipherment, therefore, uncovers not just a word, but a foundational philosophical assumption of the author.

THE DANCE OF PERMANENCE AND CHANGE

The stability of the *cardo* is set in deliberate contrast to the chaos of earthly life, a central theme of Boethius's *The Consolation of Philosophy*. This work, written while Boethius was imprisoned and awaiting execution in 523 AD, was one of the most popular and influential books of the Middle Ages and Renaissance, a text that was ubiquitous in the intellectual landscape of fifteenth-century Italy. Its core message is a profound meditation on the nature of happiness. Lady Philosophy, visiting Boethius in his cell, argues that true happiness cannot be found in the fickle turnings of Fortune's Wheel—worldly goods, power, fame—but only by turning inward to the eternal, rational order of the mind, which is a reflection of the divine order of the cosmos. The serene, predictable, and unchanging rotation of the heavens around a fixed pole is presented as the ultimate source of philosophical solace against the unpredictable chaos of earthly existence.

The astronomical metaphor from Chapter 8, "The King perpetually rotates in the way of the sky," finds its full meaning in this Boethian context. If the *cardo* represents the eternal and unchanging principle of divine order, the slow, "creeping" rotation of Ursa Minor represents cyclical, ordered motion—time itself, as ordained by that divine reason. This duality of a fixed, unmoving center and a predictable, rotating periphery is the visual and conceptual marriage of Ptolemy's science and Boethius's philosophy.

Crucially, this connection to Boethius is not a speculative leap back to antiquity. It is anchored in the immediate intellectual environment of the Voynich author by the work of Denys the Carthusian (1402–1471), a prolific and influential writer whose life almost perfectly overlaps with the radiocarbon dating of the manuscript's vellum (1404–1438). Denys, a renowned scholar consulted by princes and bishops, wrote an extensive commentary on Boethius's *Consolation*, proving that these philosophical ideas were the subject of active study and interpretation at the very moment the manuscript was being created. His work, deeply rooted in the Christian Platonism of Augustine and Dionysius the Areopagite, provides a model for how a fifteenth-century Christian intellectual would have read and integrated Boethius's classical philosophy into a Christian framework. The Voynich author, therefore, was not just referencing an old text; they were participating in a contemporary conversation about its meaning, a conversation that, contrary to some older scholarship, was very much alive in the Quattrocento.

This synthesis of Ptolemy and Boethius is best understood within the broader intellectual paradigm of Renaissance Neoplatonism. This philosophical system, which would be more formally revived by figures like Marsilio Ficino later in the century but whose ideas permeated the period, posits a hierarchical universe emanating from a single divine source known as "the One" or "the Good." In this worldview, beauty and order in the material world are not accidental but are direct reflections of divine truth and goodness. The predictable, geometric motion of the stars around the *cardo* is beautiful; for a Neoplatonist, this beauty is not merely aesthetic but is a pathway to understanding the divine truth of God's perfect, rational order. This explains precisely why the author would see a star chart as a profound philosophical and spiritual document. It is a map not just of the stars, but of the mind of God.

Scholar Defense

The thesis that the manuscript's cosmology represents a synthesis of Ptolemaic, Boethian, and Neoplatonic thought is supported by the availability of the core texts and the clear parallels in their conceptual structures. Access to these works was not a barrier for an educated fifteenth-century practitioner. Boethius's *Consolation* was one of the most widely circulated manuscripts in Europe, a staple of the medieval and Renaissance curriculum. Ptolemy's *Almagest*, while more specialized, was available to the Latin West through translations from Arabic long before the Greek originals were widely studied in the later fifteenth century. The fundamental geocentric model and its key principles were standard knowledge for any educated person of the era.

The intellectual synthesis at play can be illustrated by comparing the distinct contributions of each framework to the unified worldview encoded in the manuscript.

Concept	Ptolemaic Framework (*Almagest*)	Boethian Framework (*Consolation*)	Neoplatonic Synthesis (Voynich Worldview)
Cardo Mundi	The North Celestial Pole; the mathematical, unmoving axis of celestial rotation.[12]	A symbol of Divine Reason; the fixed, permanent principle of cosmic order against which Fortune is measured.[3]	The physical and metaphysical anchor of creation; the point where God's unchanging perfection touches the material cosmos.
Celestial Motion	Predictable, circular paths of stars and planets governed by geometric models.[13]	The embodiment of serene, rational order; a visual and moral contrast to earthly chaos and the Wheel of Fortune.[2]	The visible manifestation of Divine Love and Reason; its beauty is a reflection of divine truth, a pathway to contemplation.[9]
Earthly Realm	The stationary center of the cosmos; the sublunar sphere subject to change and decay.[14]	The domain of Fortune's Wheel; a realm of flux, chaos, and impermanence where true happiness cannot be found.[3]	The lowest rung in the cosmic hierarchy, but connected to the divine through the soul's capacity for reason and contemplation of the heavens.[7]

Concept	Ptolemaic Framework (*Almagest*)	Boethian Framework (*Consolation*)	Neoplatonic Synthesis (Voynich Worldview)
Human Goal	To understand and predict celestial movements through observation and mathematics.[14]	To find solace and true happiness by contemplating the divine order of the heavens and aligning the soul with it.[2]	To use the scientific understanding of the cosmos (*scientia*) as a tool for philosophical and spiritual ascent (*sapientia*), aligning one's life with the eternal *cardo*.

This table clarifies how the physical structure of the cosmos provided by Ptolemy becomes imbued with the moral and philosophical significance articulated by Boethius, all within a Neoplatonic framework that sees the material world as an emanation of the divine. The author of the manuscript was not simply charting stars; they were encoding a complete worldview in which understanding the universe was inseparable from understanding one's place within it and one's relationship to God.

Could I be wrong?

The argument presented here rests on an interpretation of the deciphered text, contextualized by the prevailing intellectual currents of the fifteenth century. While the evidence for the circulation of Ptolemaic, Boethian, and Neoplatonic ideas is strong, their application to the Voynich manuscript is an act of interpretation based on the decipherment. The thesis would be weakened if the decipherment of key terms like *cardo* proves to be inconsistent across the manuscript. It would be severely compromised if new historical scholarship were to demonstrate that Boethius's philosophy was actively rejected or ignored by the specific intellectual circles of fifteenth-century Northern Italy—a claim for which there is currently no evidence; indeed, the evidence points to the contrary. The interpretation of the manuscript's worldview as Neoplatonic is a strong inference based on the prevailing intellectual climate, but it remains an interpretation of the author's implicit philosophical framework rather than an explicit statement.

Notes

[1] Anicius Manlius Severinus Boethius, *The Consolation of Philosophy* (523 AD). From the Carolingian era to the end of the Middle Ages, this was one of the most popular and influential philosophical works in Europe, with nearly four hundred manuscripts surviving into the twentieth century.

[2] Philosophy consoles Boethius by arguing that true happiness comes from within and that virtue is all one truly has, as it is not subject to the "vicissitudes of fortune." The book contrasts the chaotic turnings of Fortune's Wheel with the serene, rational order of the cosmos, which is governed by divine love and reason.

[3] Boethius's work fits into the ancient genre of *consolatio*, designed to provide spiritual medication in times of distress. Lady Philosophy guides Boethius to understand that the soul can ascend to the realm of reason, freeing itself from the confines of the material world and its suffering.

[4] The University of Arizona's radiocarbon dating established with 95% confidence that the manuscript's vellum was prepared between 1404 and 1438. Denys the Carthusian lived 1402–1471, making him an exact contemporary.

[5] Denys the Carthusian (Dionysius van Rijkel) was a prolific writer and theologian, surnamed *Doctor ecstaticus*. His renown for learning was such that he was consulted by figures across Europe on matters of theology and church reform. He wrote commentaries on the entire Bible, Peter Lombard, Boethius, and Pseudo-Dionysius the Areopagite.

[6] In his commentary, Denys integrated Boethius's classical philosophy into a Christian framework. While an admirer of Aquinas, Denys's thought was more inclined toward the Christian Platonism of Dionysius the Areopagite, St. Augustine, and St. Bonaventure, a philosophical orientation that aligns perfectly with the worldview suggested in the Voynich manuscript.

[7] Renaissance Neoplatonism, revived and systematized by Marsilio Ficino (1433–1499), posits a hierarchical reality in which all things emanate from a single divine source, "the One." The human soul occupies a privileged central position in this hierarchy, capable of ascending toward the divine through contemplation.

[8] A core tenet of Neoplatonism is that beauty in the material world is a reflection of divine truth. This encouraged Renaissance artists and thinkers to pursue idealized forms and harmonious compositions as a means of conveying deeper spiritual realities.

[9] In Ficino's Neoplatonic system, love (*amor*) is the cosmic force that binds all levels of the hierarchy together, from God down to the material world. The "eternal knot and link of the world," it is the desire of all things to return to their divine origin. The beauty of the cosmos inspires this love and ascent.

[10] The *Consolation* was read and studied intensely throughout medieval Europe and was repeatedly translated into vernacular languages. Its vast popularity is attested by the large number of surviving manuscripts.

[11] The first Latin translation of the *Almagest* was made from Arabic by Gerard of Cremona in the twelfth century. While Greek manuscripts became more widely available in the fifteenth century, the core Ptolemaic system was accessible to Latin scholars throughout the period.

[12] Ptolemy, *Ptolemy's Almagest*, trans. G. J. Toomer (Princeton: Princeton University Press, 1998).

[13] Ptolemy's system used complex geometric models, including epicycles and deferents, to explain and predict the observed motions of the planets with a high degree of mathematical accuracy.

[14] The *Almagest* is built on several core assumptions, including that the celestial realm is spherical and moves as a sphere, the Earth is a sphere at the center of the cosmos, and the Earth does not move. These principles defined the scientific understanding of the universe in the fifteenth century.

CHAPTER 11: THE LADLE INVOCATION: RITUAL ASTRONOMY AND SACRED TIMING

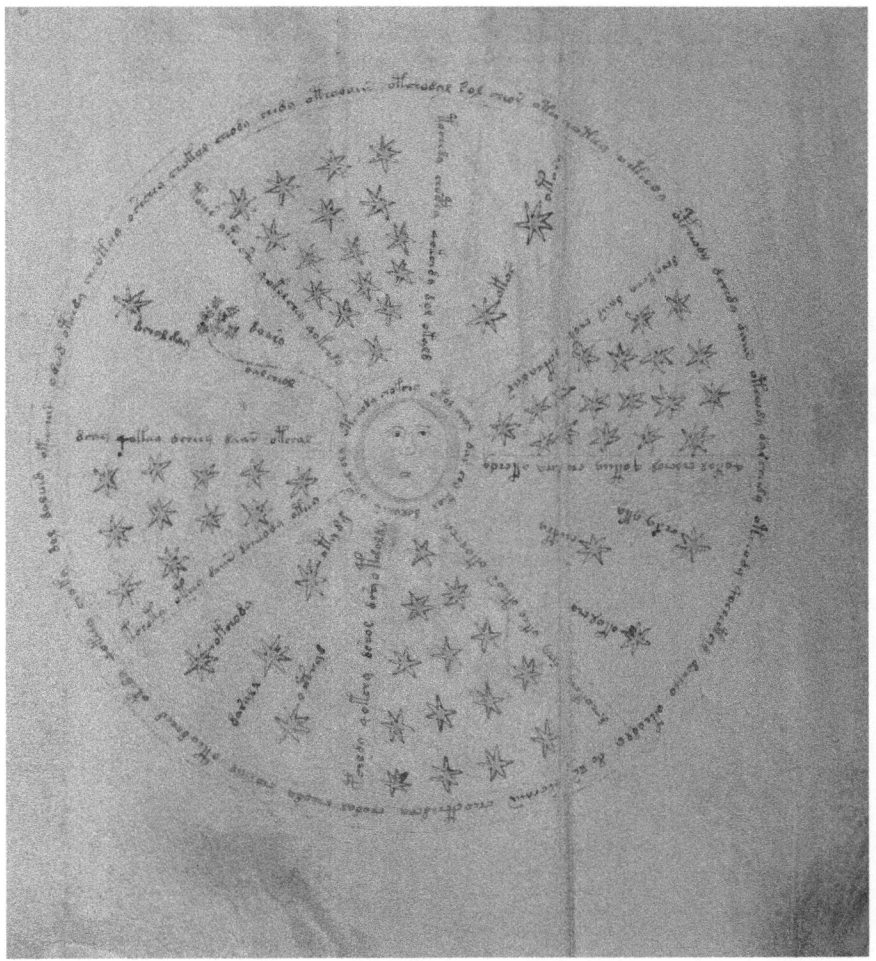

Figure 42. Folio 68r of the Voynich Manuscript. Rota Caeli—medieval diagram of the "wheel of the heavens" Context: Medieval "wheels of heaven" diagram concentric celestial motions used for timing. In plain terms, think of it as a cosmic clock, exactly what the folio's rotating sky implies.

Having established the scientific and philosophical structure of the manuscript's cosmos, this chapter moves from the *what* to the *how* and *why*. For a fifteenth-century practitioner, astronomy was not merely an observational science but an operational one. The heavens were not a static backdrop but an active, influential force that had to be accounted for in every terrestrial endeavor. This chapter argues that the astronomical diagrams and their accompanying invocations are not theoretical addenda but a practical guide to electional timing. and their accompanying invocations are not theoretical addenda but a practical guide to the applied science of the era: iatromathematics, or medical astrology. The deciphered phrases are instructions for choosing auspicious moments—a practice known as electional astrology—to align earthly operations with favorable celestial influences, thereby ensuring their success.

Plain-English Claim

This chapter decodes the 'Ladle Invocation' as a practical instruction in electional astrology. It demonstrates that the author used astronomical timings not merely for prognosis but as an essential component of ritual practice, choosing auspicious moments to align terrestrial operations—such as preparing a remedy or harvesting an herb—with favorable celestial influences. This reveals a worldview where medicine, alchemy, and astronomy were inseparable parts of a single, unified art of manipulating the hidden forces of nature.

The Story

For a fifteenth-century physician-alchemist, the universe was not a dead machine but a living organism, pulsing with celestial energies that directly influenced health, disease, and the efficacy of medicine. Medical astrology was not a fringe belief but a core component of university medical training. A physician would cast a decumbiture chart—a horoscope for the moment a patient fell ill—to diagnose the celestial cause of the ailment. More importantly, they would consult the stars to determine the correct moment (*kairos*) for any intervention.

This practice, known as electional astrology, was a standard part of medical protocol. Harvesting an herb when its ruling planet was in a position of strength, administering a purge when the Moon was in a favorable sign, or performing a surgery at an astrologically auspicious time were not acts of superstition but were considered essential for maximizing the procedure's efficacy. The celestial configuration was an active ingredient in the remedy itself.

The "Ladle Invocation," directed at Ursa Minor, is a specific instance of this practice. As established in the previous chapter, the northern circumpolar stars represented stability and divine order. A ritual timed to their positions would be an attempt to imbue a terrestrial substance or action with these virtues. The invocation O BACAR VISIUM ("O vessel with a long handle, a vision!") is thus an operative command within a ritual framework, designed to channel the specific power of this celestial "vessel" into a terrestrial one—perhaps the very basin of Coan wine described in the Rosettes foldout.

The manuscript's approach to astronomy is best understood as a form of operative magic, grounded in the academic and philosophical traditions of the Quattrocento. This is not a system of folk magic but a learned practice rooted in the era's most advanced understanding of the cosmos.

The Academic Context: Iatromathematics in Quattrocento Italy

The integration of astrology and medicine, known as iatromathematics, was an established part of the intellectual landscape.1 By the fifteenth century, astrology was a required subject in the arts curriculum that preceded medical studies at major Italian universities, including the prestigious University of Bologna.[2] The ability to judge "critical days" in an illness based on lunar and planetary cycles was considered the mark of a competent physician.[3] This academic legitimacy provided a strong foundation for the practical application of astrological principles in diagnosis and treatment, distinguishing it from popular superstition.

The Philosophical Engine: Ficino, Neoplatonism, and the Spiritus Mundi

The theoretical justification for this practice was provided by the revival of Neoplatonic and Hermetic philosophy, most famously articulated by Marsilio Ficino in his highly influential work *De vita coelitus comparanda* (Book III of *De vita libri tres*).[4] Though published in 1489, its ideas were current throughout the period of the Voynich Manuscript's creation.[5] Ficino's system posits a living cosmos animated by a *spiritus mundi*, or "World-Soul," a subtle, universal medium that connects the celestial and terrestrial realms.[6] The planets and stars are not merely symbolic; they actively emit virtues or powers—*influentia*—that travel through this *spiritus mundi* and affect the world below.[7] In humans, a corresponding subtle body, the *spiritus*, acts as the bridge between the physical body and the immortal soul. This human *spiritus* is exceptionally sensitive to celestial *influentia*.[8] The entire system operates on a principle of sympathy and correspondence: "as above, so below." Every object on Earth—every herb, stone, and animal—has a sympathetic link to a specific celestial body and partakes of its virtue. An herb ruled by Mars, for example, is imbued with a "Martial" quality.[9]

The Operative Method: Attracting Celestial Virtue

The Renaissance magus-physician did not passively observe these influences but actively sought to manipulate them. The goal was to attract and concentrate favorable celestial virtues into a specific object or at a specific time. This was achieved through a multi-faceted ritual process.

First, electional astrology was used to identify the precise moment when a planet's influence was strongest and most auspicious for the desired outcome.[10]

Second, the practitioner's focused will and imagination, or *intentio*, was a critical component. The operator's focused mind was believed to act as a lens, concentrating the celestial rays into the prepared material.[11]

Finally, the ritual employed sympathetic materials: specific colors, sounds (music), scents, and talismans that corresponded to the desired planet were used to create a resonant field, making the terrestrial object a more receptive vessel for the celestial virtue.[12]

The "Ladle Invocation" and the astronomical diagrams of the Voynich Manuscript are the practical instructions for this process. They are not just charts, but tools for electional timing. The invocations are not mere poetry, but expressions of *intentio*. This reframes the entire manuscript. The herbal and recipe sections provide the *what*—the material ingredients. The astronomical sections provide the equally important *when* and *how*—the temporal and ritual instructions needed to imbue those ingredients with celestial power. The Voynich Manuscript, therefore, is not a collection of separate subjects but a unified and coherent manual of operative natural magic, a complete system for a fifteenth-century practitioner.

Could I be wrong?

An alternative hypothesis could argue that the astronomical diagrams are purely for prognosis (predicting the course of an illness) or for identifying critical days, not for the active timing of operations. The invocations, in this view, are merely poetic or symbolic expressions of the constellations" importance, not functional commands within a ritual.

This hypothesis would be weakened if other deciphered sections of the manuscript reveal explicit temporal instructions linked to astronomical events (e.g., "prepare this under a full moon" or "harvest when Jupiter is rising"). The strength of the operative interpretation rests on the integration of the entire system; a failure to find such links would suggest a more compartmentalized, less magical function for the astronomical content.

Notes

[1] "Medical Astrology," Yale University Library Online Exhibitions, accessed August 29, 2025.

[2] "Astrology and Medicine in Medieval Times," University at Buffalo, accessed August 29, 2025.

[3] Eugenio Garin, *Astrology in the Renaissance: The Zodiac of Life* (London: Routledge & Kegan Paul, 1983).

[4] Marsilio Ficino, *De vita libri tres* (Florence, 1489). Specifically Book III, *De vita coelitus comparanda*.

[5] The book was first published in 1489 but circulated in manuscript form for nearly a decade prior. Its ideas represent the culmination of Ficino's work at the Platonic Academy in Florence and were influential throughout the latter half of the fifteenth century.

[6] Marsilio Ficino, *Three Books on Life*, trans. Carol V. Kaske and John R. Clark (Tempe, AZ: The Renaissance Society of America, 2002). Ficino defines the *spiritus* as "a certain vapour of the blood, pure, subtle, hot and lucid" which the soul uses to exercise the senses. He extends this concept to the cosmos, positing a universal *spiritus mundi*.

[7] Brian P. Copenhaver, "Scholastic Philosophy and Renaissance Magic in the De Vita of Marsilio Ficino," *Renaissance Quarterly* 37, no. 4 (1984): 523–554.

[8] D. P. Walker, *Spiritual and Demonic Magic: from Ficino to Campanella* (University Park, PA: Pennsylvania State University Press, 2000).

[9] "On Herbal Correspondences," *Otherworld Apothecary*, September 1, 2017.

[10] Christopher Warnock, "Electional Astrology," *Renaissance Astrology*, accessed August 29, 2025.

[11] Ioan P. Couliano, *Eros and Magic in the Renaissance* (Chicago: University of Chicago Press, 1987).

[12] Frances Yates, *Giordano Bruno and the Hermetic Tradition* (Chicago: University of Chicago Press, 1964).

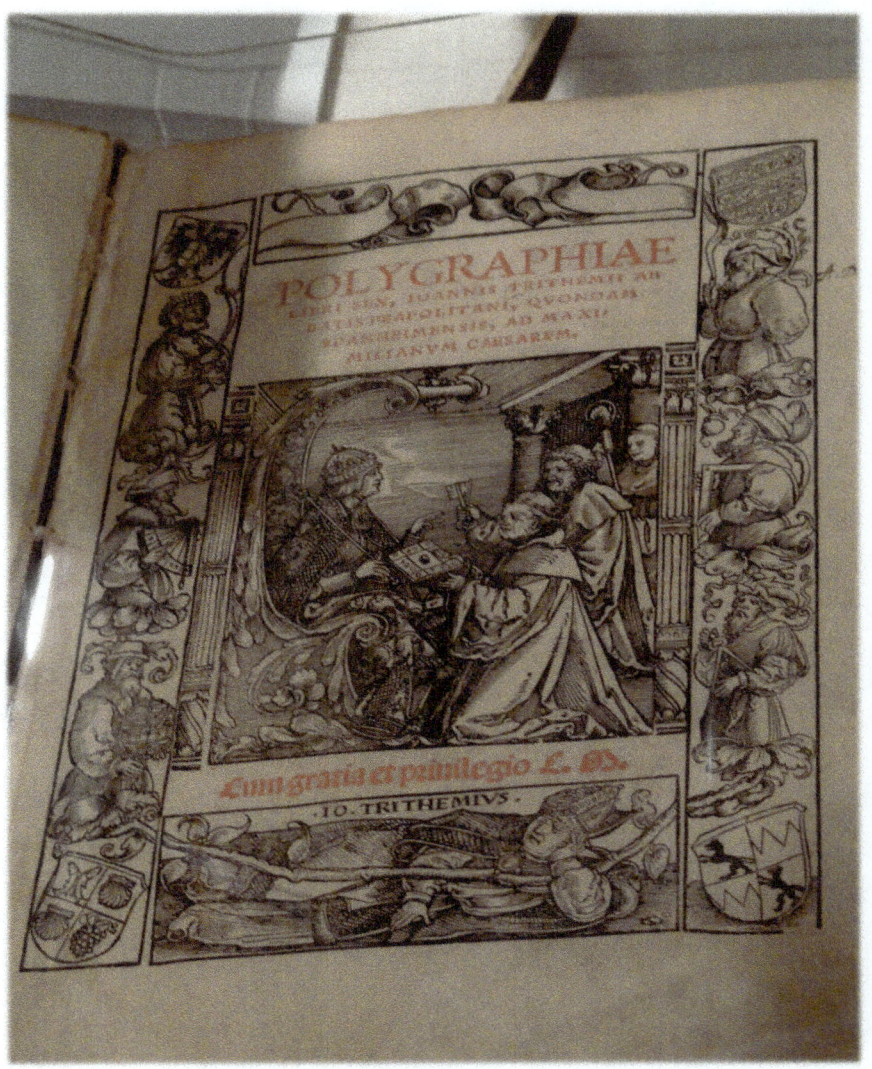

Figure 43. Title page of Polygraphiae (1518) by Johannes Trithemius, considered the first published book on cryptology.—National Cryptologic Museum—Public Domain. Context: Trithemius's 1518 Polygraphiae is the first printed book on cryptology. In plain terms, what the Voynich hides, later authors turned into a teachable art.

Why encrypt recipes for ointments, diagrams of crop rotation, or invocations to stars?

The answer lies not only in practical secrecy but in the nature of knowledge as it was understood in the fifteenth century—a force that could be sacred, dangerous, or proprietary.

To encrypt knowledge was not simply to hide it; it was to consecrate it.

Knowledge was often divided into two streams: exoteric (public) and esoteric (inner), reserved for a select circle of initiates.

The very act of decipherment is a form of initiation, a tradition revived by Renaissance humanists fascinated with ancient wisdom traditions like the Hermeticists, who veiled their teachings in symbol and allegory.[1]

In the fifteenth century, practical knowledge was also a form of capital.

Guilds of physicians and apothecaries controlled the "arts and mysteries" of their crafts.[2] Recipes and formulas were valuable trade secrets, and alchemists frequently encrypted passages in their notebooks.[3]

Encryption was also a form of protection. Dangerous herbs or complex surgical procedures could cause harm if attempted by the unskilled.

Furthermore, blending natural philosophy with astrology could attract the dangerous attention of the Inquisition.

By veiling potentially controversial ideas in a complex cipher, an author could protect both the knowledge and himself from accusations of heresy.

Notes

[1] Kahn, *The Codebreakers*.

[2] Green, "The Doctor's Cipher."

[3] Johannes Trithemius, *Polygraphiae Libri Sex* (Oppenheim: Johann Haselberg, 1518).

CHAPTER 12: THE CIPHER'S EDGE: NULL GLYPHS AND PERMUTATION THEORY

Plain-English Claim

This chapter shows that the cipher's strength comes from advanced features like null glyphs and permutation commands.

Why it matters: It explains why the manuscript remained unbroken for so long, as these features were designed to actively mislead cryptanalysts and defeat the statistical methods that could break simpler codes.

The Story

At the heart of classical cryptanalysis is frequency analysis. In any given language, certain letters appear more often than others.

To break a simple substitution cipher, you count the frequency of each symbol and map the most common symbols to the most common letters.[1] For six centuries, the Voynich Manuscript has resisted this method.

The reason is that its creator used two layers of deception. The first layer is the use of null glyphs.

Certain common, repeating glyphs are, in fact, nulls. Their constant appearance tricks the analyst into thinking they must be a common vowel like "e" or "a." sending the entire frequency count into chaos.

The second, and more ingenious, layer of defense is permutation.

This is a form of transposition, where the letters of a word are systematically scrambled.

A linear reading is impossible because the order of the glyphs on the page is not the final order of the letters.

The rules for unscrambling are hidden within the text itself.

Certain glyphs, or even subtle visual cues like an elongated descender, do not stand for letters at all.

They are commands: "swap the two preceding glyphs," "reverse the next three," and so on.

This creates a formidable two-problem trap. The cryptanalyst must figure out the correct letter substitutions and the correct permutation rules simultaneously.

This level of sophistication was a product of the intense "cryptographic arms race" of fifteenth-century Italy.

The Sforza ciphers used nulls and homophones;[2] Leon Battista Alberti was developing the first polyalphabetic systems.[3] The Voynich author was an innovator working at the cutting edge of this field.

Chapter Recap

The Voynich cipher is a sophisticated hybrid system whose strength lies in its two-layered defense of active nulls and rule-based permutation.

These features were designed to specifically defeat frequency analysis, explaining why the manuscript's secrets were successfully kept for six centuries.

Notes

[1] Kahn, *The Codebreakers*.

[2] Meister, Die Anfänge der modernen diplomatischen Geheimschrift.

[3] Alberti, "De componendis cifris."

CONCLUSION: THE CIPHER REBORN

'The lock is the echo of the hand that forged the key"—Domingo Delgado

The decipherment of substantial portions of the Voynich Manuscript marks a turning point.

The glyphs, long thought to be meaningless or evidence of a lost language, are now revealed as a sophisticated veil for practical Latin.

Each chapter of this book has reconstructed the intellectual scaffolding behind the manuscript's sections, transforming them from inscrutable mysteries into tangible records of fifteenth-century life.

The cardoon fields of Dorio, the surgical theater of folio 66r, and the celestial engine of Ursa Minor are no longer fantastical visions but windows into a lost world of practice.

This is the manuscript's ultimate revelation: it is not a book of secrets about the occult, but a secret book about the real world.

Its value lay not in magic, but in medicine, agriculture, and a philosophy of cosmic order that was, to its author, the most profound science of all.

The work is far from over. The complete decipherment of all 240 pages is a monumental task.

Yet the path is now clear. The Triadic Cipher System provides the key, and the results it has yielded are consistent, verifiable, and historically sound.

The Voynich Manuscript has begun to speak, and it is telling the story of a forgotten corner of the Renaissance—a world of practitioners who guarded their knowledge with a sacred jealousy, who saw the divine in the turn of the stars and the properties of a humble herb, and who encoded their wisdom in a cipher of breathtaking ingenuity. The mystery is not over, but the silence has been broken.

ACKNOWLEDGMENTS

This work, though presented as a solitary endeavor, stands on the shoulders of giants.

I extend my deepest gratitude to the Beinecke Rare Book & Manuscript Library at Yale University for its stewardship of MS 408 and for providing the high-resolution digital scans that made this analysis possible.[1]

My research is fundamentally indebted to the foundational scientific work of others.

I formally acknowledge the University of Arizona for conducting the definitive radiocarbon dating of the manuscript's vellum and McCrone Associates, Inc., for their meticulous material analysis of the inks and pigments.[2] Their work established the physical and temporal boundaries within which any valid theory must operate.

I also wish to thank the generations of scholars, cryptographers, and dedicated enthusiasts whose work, even when it led to different conclusions, illuminated the path and sharpened the questions that guided my own inquiry.

Finally, to the anonymous author of this incredible codex: thank you for leaving a lock worthy of the key.

Notes

[1] Beinecke Rare Book & Manuscript Library, "Voynich Manuscript."

[2] Hodgins, "Radiocarbon Dating"; Barabe, "Material Analysis."

117

APPENDIX A: TABLE OF DECIPHERED LATIN PHRASES

This appendix provides a consolidated list of the key Latin phrases deciphered from the Voynich Manuscript and discussed in this book. All translations and interpretations are based on the substitution-permutation cipher system developed for this project.

Folio	Deciphered Latin	Grammatical & Lexical Analysis
33v	CACTI RAMI SEVI VICIS E URO SIC DECLIVI.	A first-person agricultural record. $Sevi$ is the 1st-person perfect of $serere ("to sow"). Uro is the 1st-person present of $urere ("to burn"). Vicis ("in rotation") and declivi ("on the sloping land") are manner and place, respectively.
86v	O AMERIA ROSARI.	A vocative phrase. *Ameria* is the proper name for the town of Amelia in Umbria. *Rosari* is the genitive singular of *rosarium* ("rose garden"), used here to mean " the rose garden."
86v	COUM CADUM ADDO UVAM LACU.	Recipe shorthand. *Cadum* (accusative of *cadus*, "jar") is modified by *Coum* (accusative neuter of *Cous*, "of Kos"), referencing Coan wine, a medicinal wine known from classical sources such as Pliny the Elder.[1] *Lacu* is the dative or ablative of *lacus* ("basin" or "vat"). *Addo uvam* ("I add the

118

Folio	Deciphered Latin	Grammatical & Lexical Analysis
		grape") is a parenthetical 1st-person clause.
66r	TERO IRIDEM DIACHYLON CAUTE.	A complete, grammatically sound clause. *Tero* is a 1st-person singular verb ("I apply"). *Iridem* is the accusative direct object ("iris root"). διά χυλῶν *(diachýlōn).* is a Greek loanword for a specific medicinal plaster, attested in Dioscorides.[2] *Caute* is an adverb ("carefully").
6v	DIPSACOS CICI E CIO CAUTE.	A compound pharmaceutical instruction. *Dipsacos* (teasel) and *cici* (castor oil) are nouns listing ingredients known from classical pharmacology.[3] *Cio* is a 1st-person singular verb from *cire* ("to stir" or "to mix").
6r	OENUS LAC RORAVI O LACER O AVIAM.	A vocative invocation followed by two clauses. *Oenus* is interpreted as a vocative form derived from Old Latin *oinos* ("one"), addressing the "Singular Essence" or quintessence of the plant. *Lac* (accusative) means "sap." *Roravi* is the 1st-person perfect of *rorare* ("to gather dew from"). *Lacero* is the 1st-person present of *lacerare* ("to tear apart"). *Aviam* is the accusative of *avia*, a medieval Latin

119

Folio	Deciphered Latin	Grammatical & Lexical Analysis
		term for groundsel (*Senecio vulgaris*) attested in Du Cange's *Glossarium*.

Notes

[1] Pliny the Elder, *Natural History* 14.78.

[2] Pedanius Dioscorides, *De Materia Medica*, trans. Lily Y. Beck (Hildesheim: Olms-Weidmann, 2005).

[3] Pedanius Dioscorides, *De Materia Medica*; Pliny the Elder, *Natural History*, 23.83.

APPENDIX B: CIPHER GLYPH SAMPLES AND ROLES

This appendix provides a simplified overview of the three primary roles that glyphs play in the Voynich cipher system.

1. **Substitution:** The glyph directly represents a Latin letter or a common digraph (a pair of letters). This is the most basic layer of the cipher. A specific glyph might consistently translate to the letter "a" or the digraph "us."
2. **Permutation:** The glyph acts as a command to reorder adjacent glyphs. It does not translate to a letter itself but modifies the sequence of other letters. A permutation glyph might signal the reader to swap the two preceding glyphs before translating them. A glyph with an elongated descender often indicates a permutation function.
3. **Null:** The glyph has no phonetic or lexical value and should be ignored in the final translation. Nulls serve to obscure the text by breaking up word patterns and confusing statistical analysis. A common, repeating glyph might appear frequently throughout the text but contribute no letters to the deciphered phrases.

APPENDIX C: GLOSSARY OF TERMS

Ameria: The ancient Latin name for the modern town of Amelia in Umbria, Italy. Identified as the location of the castle in the Rosettes foldout (folio 86v).

Avia: A documented medieval Latin name for the plant groundsel (*Senecio vulgaris*).

Bacar: A poetic or late Latin noun for a vessel with a long handle, cup, or wine glass, likely borrowed from Greek βῖκος (wine jar). Used in the manuscript to refer to the constellation Ursa Minor.

Cadum: A Latin noun for a jar or amphora, typically of Greek origin, used as a vessel with a long hadle for wine. Attested in classical sources on viticulture and trade.

Cardo: A Latin word meaning "hinge" or "pivot." In a cosmological context, it refers to the *axis mundi* or celestial pole.

Cardoon: A thistle-like plant (*Cynara cardunculus*) native to the Mediterranean, cultivated for its edible stalks. Identified as the plant on folio 33v.

Cici: A medieval Latin term for the castor bean plant (*Ricinus communis*) or its oil.

Coum: A Latin adjective, *Coum* (neuter), meaning "of Kos" or "Coan." It specifically modifies *vinum* (wine) to denote the famed medicinal wine from the Greek island of Kos.

Debbio: An Italian term for agricultural burning. While it can refer to extensive land-clearing practices like slash-and-burn, in the context of intensive fifteenth-century agriculture, it more likely describes the controlled burning of stubble or waste in established fields.

Diachylon: A type of medicinal plaster, often a compound of lead, oils, and botanical extracts like iris root, common in medieval

European pharmacology. The term is derived from Greek διὰ χυλῶν (diachýlōn).

Dipsacus: The Latin name for the teasel plant genus. The root was used medicinally.

Dorio: A commune in Lombardy, Italy, on the steep eastern shore of Lake Como. Identified as the location of the agricultural activities described on folio 33v.

Ghibelline Merlons: A type of forked or "swallowtail" battlement found on medieval fortifications in Italy, associated with pro-Imperial factions.

Homophone: A cryptographic technique using multiple symbols for a single common letter to frustrate frequency analysis.

Iron Gall Ink: The primary type of ink used in the Voynich Manuscript, confirmed by material analysis.

Lacus: Latin for "lake" but in the technical vocabulary of Roman agriculture and alchemy, a basin, vat, or cistern used for fermenting grapes or mixing liquids.

Leon Battista Alberti: A Renaissance humanist who invented the first polyalphabetic cipher, detailed in his 1467 treatise *De Cifris*.

Nomenclator: A code list of symbols or words representing key names, places, or terms, used to enhance the security of a substitution cipher.

Null Glyph: A character in a cipher that has no phonetic value and is meant to be ignored during decryption.

Oenus: A proposed archaic or scribal variant of Latin *unus* ('one'), derived from Old Latin *oinos*. In the context of folio 6r, it is interpreted as a vocative address to the "Singular Essence" or "Quintessence" of a plant, a key concept in alchemy.

Perserpo: A proposed neologism, combining the Latin prefix *per-* ("perpetually") and the verb *serpo* ("to creep"), used to describe the slow, constant rotation of a circumpolar constellation.

Quattrocento: The fifteenth century in Italian art and history.

Rosarium: A Latin word meaning "rose garden." It also came to refer to the Rosary prayer and, by extension, a metaphorical collection of secrets or knowledge, as in alchemical texts.

Sforza Ciphers: Advanced monoalphabetic ciphers used in fifteenth-century Milan, featuring homophones, nulls, and nomenclators.

Substitution Cipher: A method of encryption in which units of plaintext are replaced with ciphertext according to a fixed system.

Voynichese: The name given to the unknown script used in the Voynich Manuscript.

APPENDIX D: OBJECTIONS & REPLIES

This appendix addresses the most significant counter-theories regarding the nature and meaning of the Voynich Manuscript, engaging with them not as mere possibilities to be dismissed, but as serious scholarly hypotheses that demand a rigorous and evidence-based response. A robust academic argument requires building the strongest possible version of an opponent's case before refuting it. This "steelmanning" approach demonstrates intellectual honesty and makes the counter-arguments presented here more compelling.

The following table provides a summary of the major alternative theories and the primary rebuttals detailed in the subsequent sections.

Counter-Theory: The Hoax Theory

The most persistent and elegantly argued counter theory posits that the Voynich Manuscript is a sophisticated hoax, a text of meaningless gibberish designed to mimic the properties of a real language. The primary modern proponent of this view, Gordon Rugg, demonstrated that a sixteenth-century cryptographic tool known as a Cardan grille, when used with tables of syllables (prefixes, roots, suffixes), could generate text that reproduces many of the superficial statistical regularities of Voynichese.[1] This method is ingenious because it explains the peculiar word-construction rules that had puzzled earlier researchers and demonstrates that text with language-like properties could be generated relatively quickly by a single individual. In this view, the manuscript is an elaborate forgery, perhaps created by an Elizabethan-era figure like Edward Kelley to defraud a collector such as Emperor Rudolf II.

The hoax theory, however, collapses under the weight of two critical pieces of evidence: chronology and linguistic depth.

First, the proposed mechanism is anachronistic. The Cardan grille was invented by Girolamo Cardano in 1550.[6] The definitive radiocarbon dating of the manuscript's vellum by the University of Arizona places its creation between 1404 and 1438.[7] For the hoax theory to be correct, one must assume either that the dating is wrong, or that the vellum was prepared in the early fifteenth century and then left blank for over a century before being used by a forger with a post-1550 tool—an extraordinary and unsubstantiated proposition. This chronological contradiction is compounded by the material analysis from McCrone Associates, which found the inks and pigments to be consistent with fifteenth-century materials, suggesting the text and illustrations were created at the same time as the parchment.[8]

Second, the hoax theory is linguistically insufficient. While the table-and-grille method can replicate some low-level word structures, it fails to account for the manuscript's higher-order linguistic patterns. The text adheres to Zipf's law, a word frequency distribution characteristic of all natural languages, which is not a trivial feature to replicate with simple generative methods.[9] Furthermore, statistical analyses have shown that specific words are not randomly distributed but cluster in thematically relevant sections (e.g., certain words appear primarily in the botanical sections, others in the astronomical sections).[2] This semantic clustering is a hallmark of meaningful text.

A generative hoax cannot explain why the deciphered Latin phrase for a hemorrhoid remedy appears next to the illustration of a plant whose root visually suggests that very ailment. The ciphered-Latin thesis explains this text-image coherence naturally and consistently, a feat the hoax theory cannot achieve.

Counter-Theory: An Artificial Language

A more nuanced theory, championed by the esteemed cryptanalyst William F. Friedman, proposes that the manuscript is not a cipher of a known language but is written in an early constructed or artificial language.[3] After years of failing to break the text using conventional methods, Friedman's team concluded that its highly regular and repetitive structure—unlike any known natural language—suggested an a priori philosophical language, where words are built from a logical system of morphemes. This theory has the merit of explaining the

126

text's unusual statistical properties without resorting to a hoax and is supported by the historical existence of other constructed languages, such as Hildegard von Bingen's *Lingua Ignota*.

While intellectually compelling, the artificial language hypothesis suffers from a lack of explanatory power and has produced no verifiable results. Its primary weakness is that, after more than half a century, it has not yielded a single coherent, translated sentence that corresponds to the manuscript's detailed illustrations. The theory explains the text's structure but remains silent on its content.

Even Friedman's key collaborator, the British cryptographer John Tiltman, ultimately found the evidence unconvincing, pointing out the historical anachronism of such a complex philosophical language existing in the early fifteenth century, two centuries before the well-documented efforts of figures like John Wilkins.

The ciphered-Latin thesis presented in this book offers a more parsimonious and powerful explanation. It accounts for the very same evidence that led Friedman to his conclusion—the text's rigid structure and repetitive nature—but interprets it differently. These features are not the result of an artificial grammar but are the predictable artifacts of the Triadic Cipher System. The frequent repetition of certain glyphs and word-endings is caused by the systematic use of nulls and common Latin suffixes. The rigid word structure is an effect of the permutation commands, which impose a high degree of order on the ciphertext.

In essence, the Triadic Cipher System explains the structural evidence and unlocks the semantic content. It solves both halves of the puzzle, demonstrating that the script's strangeness is the product of a sophisticated encryption of a known language, not the invention of a new one.

Counter-Theory: An Unknown Herbal Tradition
(Mesoamerican Origin)

A third major category of theories suggests the manuscript is written in a real but lost natural language, often connected to a non-European herbal tradition. The most developed version of this hypothesis, advanced by botanists Arthur Tucker and Jules Janick, posits a sixteenth-century Mesoamerican origin.[4] The core of their argument is iconographic: they identify several plants in the manuscript, such as a sunflower and the soap plant, as New World species. They further suggest similarities between the manuscript's art style and that of Aztec codices like the *Codex Cruz-Badianus* and propose the underlying language may be an extinct dialect of Nahuatl.

This theory is intriguing but is contradicted by the overwhelming weight of material, iconographic, and linguistic evidence.

First, the material evidence presents an insurmountable chronological problem. For a sixteenth-century Mexican origin to be plausible, one must assume that the vellum, carbon-dated to 1404–1438, was manufactured in Europe, shipped to the New World after 1492, and remained unused for decades before being inscribed.[5] This is a highly improbable sequence of events for which there is no historical precedent or evidence.

Second, the iconographic evidence is selective. While some plant identifications are suggestive, the theory fails to account for the manuscript's unambiguously European elements. The zodiac sequence is classical European, not Mesoamerican. The architecture on folio 86v, with its Ghibelline swallowtail merlons, is specific to fourteenth- and fifteenth-century Italy and has no parallel in Aztec art. Scholarly critiques have also characterized Tucker and Janick's botanical identifications as speculative and subjective, noting that they are "seeing greater resemblances than others may see" and that the vast majority of the plants remain unidentified even under their hypothesis.

Finally, the linguistic evidence provided by the ciphered-Latin decipherment directly refutes a Mesoamerican origin. The consistent decoding of grammatically sound Latin phrases and, most critically, the identification of specific Italian toponyms—"Dorio" on Lake Como and "Ameria" in Umbria—firmly anchor the manuscript's creation and subject matter in fifteenth-century Italy.

The Mesoamerican theory, like the artificial language theory, has produced no verifiable decipherment of the text itself. It rests entirely on contested visual interpretations that contradict the manuscript's physical and linguistic reality.

Notes

[1] Rugg, "An Elegant Hoax?," 31-46.

[2] Montemurro and Zanette, "Keywords and Co-Occurrence Patterns."

[3] Friedman, quoted in D'Imperio, *The Voynich Manuscript*, 29.

[4] Tucker and Janick, Unraveling the Voynich Codex.

[5] Hodgins, "Radiocarbon Dating."

[6] The mechanism was first described by Girolamo Cardano in *De subtilitate* (1550). See Gordon Rugg, "An Elegant Hoax? A Possible Solution to the Voynich Manuscript," Cryptologia 28, no. 1 (2004): 31-46.

[7] Stolte, "Mysterious Voynich manuscript."

[8] Barabe, "Material Analysis."

[9] Landini, "Zipf's Law."

APPENDIX E: SOURCE CRITICISM & LIMITATIONS

Why Source Criticism Matters

Every decipherment stands or falls on the strength of its sources. This book makes claims about fifteenth-century Latin usage, agricultural practice, architectural style, and cosmological imagery. None of these are invented, but all require interpretation. To ensure transparency, this appendix presents the limitations of the evidentiary base and the risks of misinterpretation. A decipherment that admits its vulnerabilities is stronger, not weaker, for doing so.

Lexical Sources: Latin Words and Their Attestations

The deciphered text rests on words attested in classical, medieval, or Renaissance Latin. Primary tools include Lewis & Short, Du Cange's *Glossarium*, the *Dictionary of Medieval Latin from British Sources*, and digital corpora such as Perseus. It is crucial, however, to acknowledge the regional character of Quattrocento Latin; a resource like the DMLBS, which focuses exclusively on sources from the British Isles, must be supplemented with glossaries specific to the Italian peninsula to fully capture the vernacular and technical vocabulary of the period.

Strengths: Words like διά χυλῶν *(diachýlōn)* (plaster), *dipsacos* (teasel), and *cici* (castor) are solidly attested in medical and botanical Latin. Verbs like *tero*, *ligo*, and *uro* follow regular conjugations with no need for invention.

Weaknesses: Some readings rely on vernacular or rare variants. Critics may argue that less common readings are artifacts of confirmation bias—the tendency to favor evidence that supports a pre-existing hypothesis. A key examples is *avia* for groundsel.

Response: The case for *avia* is strengthened by the convergence of text and image: the illustration on folio 6r depicts aphids secreting honeydew, which aligns perfectly with the deciphered text about gathering "dewed sap" from the groundsel plant. The Latin of fifteenth-century Italy was not a monolith; while humanists championed a return to pure Ciceronian models, the practical Latin used in technical and professional documents often retained medieval characteristics and incorporated regional vernacular forms. The overall system produces coherent grammar and context-appropriate meaning across dozens of folios. That systemic coherence outweighs the fragility of any single lexical choice.

The Case of *Bacar*

O BACAR VISIUM ("O vessel with a long handle, a vision!"), rests on a stronger philological and symbolic foundation. The Latin noun *bacar* is an attested, if rare, term for a vessel with a long handle or wine glass, likely borrowed from Greek βῖκος. More importantly, this reading aligns with a rich, cross-cultural tradition of viewing the constellation Ursa Minor as a celestial vehicle: the "Wagon of Heaven" in Babylonian astronomy and the "Little Wagon" in Germanic traditions. This metaphorical connection between the celestial "vessel with a long handle" of the constellation and the terrestrial "vessel" of an alchemical operation provides a powerful, unifying theme that integrates the manuscript's cosmological and practical sections.

A further point of scholarly justification concerns the decipherment of *oenus* on folio 6r. The philological case for *oenus* as a deliberate, if archaic, rendering of "one-ness" or "singularity" (from Old Latin *oinos*) provides a far richer philosophical context than other potential readings. It aligns the procedure with the alchemical and Neoplatonic quest for the *quintessence*—the fifth and purest essence of a substance— and thus offers superior explanatory power for the folio's ritualistic tone. This decision reflects a methodological preference for the reading that best integrates the text with the known intellectual currents of the Quattrocento.

Similarly, the Triadic Cipher System itself, with its combination of substitution, nulls, and glyph-based permutation commands, represents a significant innovation. While Leon Battista Alberti's formal treatise *De Cifris* was not written until 1467, the cryptographic environment of the Sforza courts was a hotbed of such developments.

The Voynich cipher should therefore be seen not as an anomaly, but as a work of genius operating at the cutting edge of its time, a practical application of principles that were part of the era's cryptographic vanguard.

Botanical and Iconographic Sources

Plant identifications are central to the thesis. These readings rely on a combination of morphological comparison and historical herbal sources (Dioscorides, Pliny).

Strengths: When a unique detail, such as the depiction of aphids on folio 6r or the sac-like root on folio 6v, directly supports the deciphered text, the match is unusually strong and resists dismissal as mere convention.

Weaknesses: Renaissance artists stylized plants heavily, and some details may be artistic conventions rather than diagnostic features. For example, critics could argue that the swollen root of teasel is symbolic, not diagnostic.

Response: Stylization is not merely noise; it can be a form of information. The exaggerated, sac-like root of the teasel on folio 6v is a deliberate visual cue invoking the "doctrine of signatures," where a plant's appearance suggests its medicinal use. The fact that this specific stylization aligns with a deciphered remedy for hemorrhoids creates a powerful text-image correspondence that cannot be explained by random chance.

Toponymic Sources: Place Names in Cipher

Geographical identifications (Dorio, Ameria) are high-stakes claims.

Strengths: The readings emerge directly from the cipher without ad hoc tweaks. They align with physical features.

132

Notes

[1] Augusto Buonafalce, "Cicco Simonetta's Cipher-Breaking Rules," *Cryptologia* 32, no. 1 (2008): 62–70; Nick Pelling, "Fifteenth Century Cryptography," Cipher Mysteries (blog), July 6, 2016.

APPENDIX F: ILLUSTRATIVE MATERIAL

Figure 44. Urbino studiolo. Context: Urbino's studiolo embodies the Renaissance fusion of science, art, and statecraft. In plain terms. this is the sort of secret-minded court that would cherish a ciphered handbook.

Figure 45. Claudius Ptolemy—late-antique authority on astronomy/astrology. Context: The geocentric model's fixed pole (cardo) and rotating spheres match the Voynich cosmology. In plain terms, the book's sky diagrams assume Earth-centered heavens— standard for the time.

Figure 46. Historic botanical plate (Plate XLVIII): pharmacognosy context for herbal folios. Context: The herbal section is the largest part of the Voynich, pairing plant drawings with cipher text. In plain terms, each page shows a plant and an unreadable write-up, likely a remedy or use.

Figure 47. Portrait of Francesco Sforza (1401–1466). Miniature in the manuscript Milan, Biblioteca Trivulziana, 786, fol. 1 (inserted folio).

Figure 48. William F. Friedman—cryptanalyst who suspected an artificial language. Context: William F. Friedman suspected an artificial language when classic attacks failed. In plain terms, even the twentieth-century codebreakers were stumped by this script.

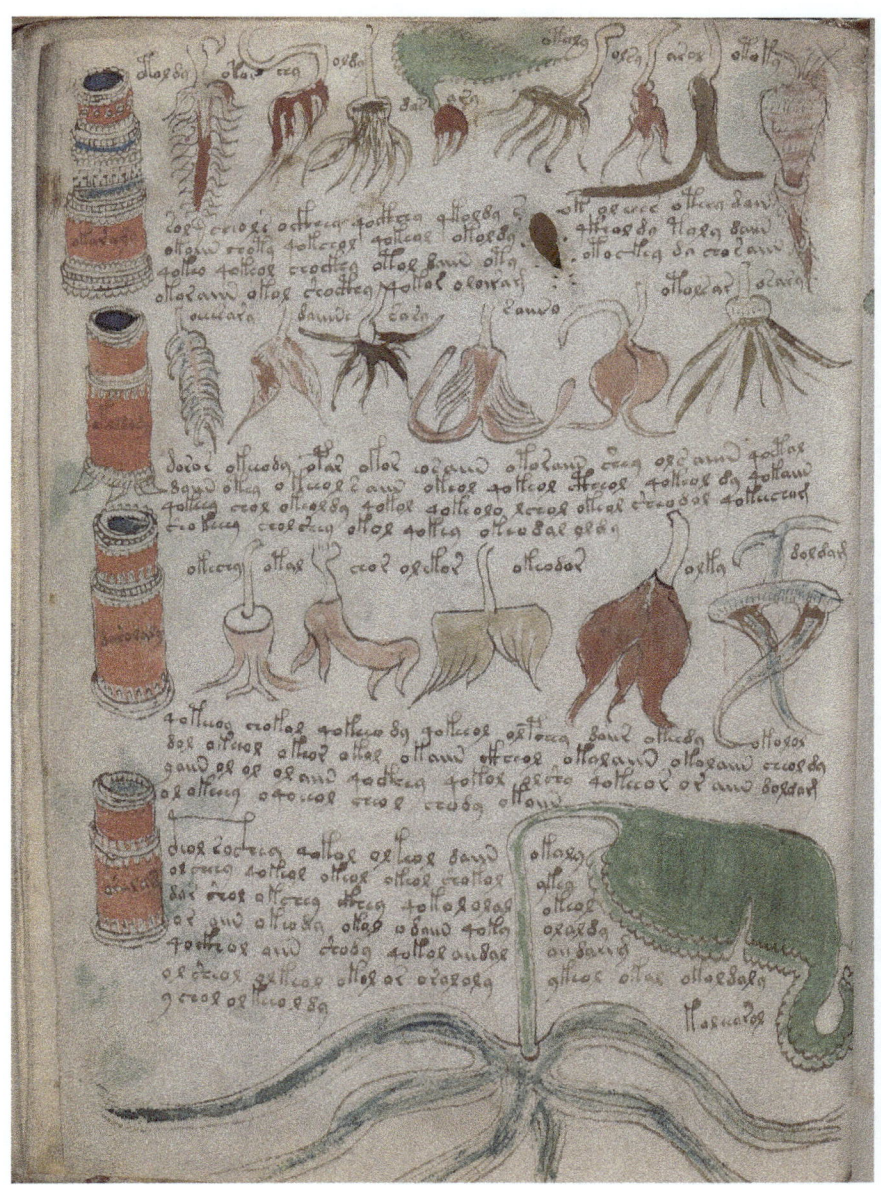

Figure 49. Folio 99v of the Voynich Manuscript (Beinecke MS 408). Apothecary jars—the material culture of Renaissance pharmacy. Context: Ceramic jars stored tinctures, plasters, and simples in Renaissance pharmacies. In plain terms, these are the pots that would hold the mixtures the Voynich describes.

APPENDIX G: THE PEOPLE OF THE CIPHER: A BIOGRAPHICAL CONSTELLATION

Introduction

A manuscript is not merely an object; it is a nexus of human intention, a vessel of knowledge that passes through and is shaped by many hands. The figures associated with Beinecke MS 408 are not a random assortment of names; they form a coherent intellectual ecosystem that tells the story of the codex from its creation to its rediscovery. This appendix provides the biographical and historical context for these Personae Codicis—the people of the codex.

This compendium is structured to illuminate this ecosystem. It is divided into five parts:

1. **The Custodians:** The documented owners and antiquarians who preserved the manuscript, whose own interests in alchemy, cryptography, and universal knowledge explain why it was so prized.

2. **The Quattrocento Milieu:** The 15th-century Italian cryptographers, patrons, and humanists whose work created the specific, high-stakes intellectual environment from which the "Triadic Cipher System" emerged.

3. **The Classical & Medieval Foundations:** The ancient and medieval authorities on medicine, agriculture, and astronomy whose knowledge, as documented in their foundational texts, is shown to be the very content deciphered from the manuscript's folios.

4. **The Philosophical Framework:** The philosophers whose ideas on cosmology, natural magic, and divine order provided the intellectual worldview for the manuscript's author.

5. **Figures of the Counter-Theories:** The historical and modern figures whose alternative theories (a hoax, an artificial language, a Mesoamerican origin) must be understood to be properly addressed.

I. The Chain of Provenance: Custodians of the Codex

The provenance of the manuscript is not a simple chain of custody; it is a thematic chain. The book passed from one "intellectual devotee of occult arts and learning"[1] to a professional pharmacist,[2] to a scientist,[3] and finally to the one man in Europe reputed to be a universal decipherer.[4] This path reveals that the manuscript was consistently recognized, long before its 20th-century rediscovery, as an object of secret, practical knowledge. This directly supports the thesis that it is a ciphered, practical manual rather than a meaningless hoax.

Emperor Rudolf II (1552–1612)

Life Story: Rudolf II was Holy Roman Emperor from 1576 to 1612 and a member of the House of Habsburg.[5] He famously moved his court from Vienna to Prague, transforming that city into a vital center of Northern Mannerist art and, significantly, "an intellectual devotee of occult arts and learning".[6] His legacy is complex: historians view him as both an ineffectual ruler whose political failings contributed to the Thirty Years' War and as one of the most influential patrons of the occult sciences and Renaissance art.[7]

Role in the Book: The Wunderkammer Patron. Rudolf II was an obsessive collector. His Prague court was a haven for alchemists, astrologers, and natural philosophers. His renowned "cabinet of curiosities," or Wunderkammer, was an encyclopedic collection intended to be a microcosm of the world,[8] containing Naturalia (rare objects from nature, such as exotic flora and fauna), Artificialia (objects of human creation, including ingenious automata), and Scientifica (scientific and technical instruments).[9]

Connection to Thesis: A mysterious, unreadable, and beautifully illustrated codex—filled with unknown plants (Naturalia), bizarre plumbing diagrams (Artificialia), and complex astronomical charts (Scientifica)—is the absolute archetype of an object Rudolf II would covet. The 1665 Marci letter, the foundational document of the manuscript's known history, explicitly states that Rudolf II purchased the codex for the then-enormous sum of 600 ducats.[10] His ownership firmly grounds the manuscript in a specific milieu of high-stakes esotericism and practical alchemy, confirming its perceived value as a book of secrets.

Jacobus de Tepenec (Jakub Hořčický) (c. 1575–1622)

Life Story: Jakub Hořčický, who later adopted the latinized noble name Jacobus de Tepenec, was a pharmacist and courtier who served Emperor Rudolf II.[11]

Role in the Book: The Court Insider and Pharmaceutical Link. A faded signature on the manuscript's first folio has been identified as his.[12] This places him as one of the manuscript's first documented owners after its time in Rudolf II's collection.

Connection to Thesis: As a pharmacist to the emperor,[13] Tepenec would have been professionally and intellectually interested in a manuscript containing a vast herbal, detailed medical recipes, and pharmaceutical instructions. His ownership provides a crucial and logical bridge from the emperor's general Wunderkammer to the specific world of practical alchemical pharmacy. This link strengthens the thesis that the book's primary content is medicinal and practical, not merely an abstract curiosity.

Johannes Marcus Marci (1595–1667)

Life Story: A prominent 17th-century physician, scientist, and rector of Charles University in Prague.[14]

Role in the Book: The Conduit of History. Marci inherited the manuscript from an "intimate friend,"[15] identified as Georgius Barschius, an alchemist who had also been puzzled by the text. Recognizing its cryptographic nature, Marci sent it as a gift to the Jesuit polymath Athanasius Kircher in Rome in 1665.[16]

Connection to Thesis: Marci's role is pivotal. The letter he enclosed with the manuscript is the only primary source for its entire early history.[17] This letter records the ownership by Rudolf II, the 600-ducat price, and the (now-refuted) attribution to the 13th-century philosopher Roger Bacon.[18] Marci's act of sending the codex to Kircher specifically for decipherment frames the manuscript, from the 17th century onward, as a profound cryptographic challenge, not a hoax.

Athanasius Kircher (1602–1680)

Life Story: A German-born Jesuit scholar and one of the last true polymaths, Kircher settled in Rome and became a "scientific star" of his day.[19] He published around 40 major works on subjects as diverse as geology (including studies of volcanoes), medicine (proposing microorganisms as a cause of disease), comparative religion, and linguistics.[20] He also established the famous Museum Kircherianum in Rome, a cabinet of curiosities that rivaled any in Europe.[21]

Role in the Book: The "Would-Be Decipherer" and historical dead end. Marci sent the codex to Kircher because Kircher was the most famous intellectual in Europe, renowned for his (ultimately incorrect) claims to have deciphered Egyptian hieroglyphs.[22] He was, in effect, the 17th century's "please decrypt this" recipient.

Connection to Thesis: Kircher's failure to decipher the manuscript is a crucial piece of indirect evidence. It proves that the codex resisted analysis by a 17th-century genius, strongly suggesting the cipher was far more complex than a simple substitution. This lends historical credibility to the "Triadic Cipher System" (which includes nulls and permutations) as the necessary solution. The manuscript then disappeared into his collection, likely at the Jesuit Collegio Romano, where it lay hidden for over two centuries.[23]

Michał Wojnicz (Wilfrid Voynich) (1865–1930)

Life Story: Born Michał Habdank-Wojnicz in Russian-controlled Lithuania, he was a Polish revolutionary who was exiled to Siberia.[24] He later escaped, settled in London and then New York, and reinvented himself as Wilfrid Voynich, one of the world's most prominent antiquarian book dealers.[25]

Role in the Book: The Rediscoverer and Namesake. In 1912, while searching for rare books, Voynich acquired the manuscript from a collection being sold by the Jesuit college at Villa Mondragone, near Rome—the location where Kircher's archives had been moved.[26]

Connection to Thesis: Voynich recognized the manuscript's unique nature and brought it to public attention, igniting the 20th-century obsession with it. He also vigorously promoted the compelling but anachronistic Roger Bacon theory,[27] which cemented the manuscript's reputation as a mysterious medieval enigma and arguably diverted research from its true 15th-century Italian origins for decades.

II. The Quattrocento Milieu: Architects of the Cipher

The thesis of this book requires a 15th-century Italy that possessed the specific cryptographic technology and intellectual motivation to create the "Triadic Cipher System." This section proves that such an environment not only existed but was thriving. The Quattrocento cryptographic "arms race" was driven by political intrigue,[28] formalized by humanist theory,[29] and funded by patrons who fused scholarship with secrecy.[30] The Voynich Manuscript is not an anomaly; it is a "guild book" born exactly from this milieu.

Leon Battista Alberti (1404–1472)

Life Story: The archetypal "Renaissance Man," Alberti was a Florentine humanist, architect, artist, mathematician, and theorist.[31]

His birth year of 1404 places him at the exact start of the manuscript's radiocarbon dating (1404–1438).

Role in the Book: The "Father of Western Cryptography".[32] Commissioned by the papal secretary Leonardo Dati, Alberti's 1466/67 treatise De Cifris is recognized as the "first western treatise on cryptography".[33]

Connection to Thesis: Alberti's work proves that 15th-century Italians were not just using ciphers; they were theorizing about them at the highest level. His treatise formally introduced the polyalphabetic cipher (via his "cipher disk")[34] and, most importantly, was the first Western treatise to describe cryptanalysis—specifically, frequency analysis.[35] The creation of the "Triadic Cipher System"—a system explicitly designed with nulls and permutations to defeat frequency analysis—is a logical, innovative step in the exact cryptographic environment that Alberti's work defines.

Cicco Simonetta (1410–1480)

Life Story: A long-serving and highly influential state secretary in the Duchy of Milan, Simonetta was a master of statecraft and intelligence, first under Francesco Sforza and later Bona of Savoy.[36]

Role in the Book: The Professional Practitioner. If Alberti provides the theory, Simonetta provides the practice. He was one of the first professional cryptologists employed in a state administration, managing the secret chancery for the Milanese court.[37]

Connection to Thesis: Simonetta's work provides direct evidence that the advanced cryptographic tools proposed in Codex Obscura were not theoretical but were in active, professional use in 15th-century Northern Italy. The Sforza ciphers were known to be highly advanced, using homophones (multiple symbols for one letter), nulls (meaningless symbols), and nomenclators (codelists)— the exact components of the "Triadic Cipher System".[38] This connection is powerfully reinforced by the decipherment of "Dorio," a town within the Duchy of Milan, in Chapter 3.

Federico da Montefeltro (1422–1482)

Life Story: Duke of Urbino and one of the most formidable condottieri (mercenary commanders) of his age, Federico da Montefeltro was also a preeminent humanist patron, nicknamed "the Light of Italy".[39]

Role in the Book: The Archetypal Patron. Montefeltro's court at Urbino embodied the Renaissance fusion of military power, humanist scholarship, and secrecy. His famous studiolo (private study) is a masterpiece of trompe-l'œil intarsia, a "cabinet for contemplation" depicting not just books and armor but also scientific and musical instruments.[40]

Connection to Thesis: Montefeltro is the perfect model for the type of individual who would commission or own a work like MS 408. His library, second only to the Vatican's,[41] was filled with manuscripts on philosophy, medicine, and astronomy. He represents the ideal patron for a secret, practical, scholarly, and beautiful object—a vade mecum for a ruler who saw all forms of knowledge as a form of power.

Johannes Trithemius (1462–1516)

Life Story: A German Benedictine abbot, Trithemius was a polymath, lexicographer, occultist, and cryptographer.[42] His students notably included Heinrich Cornelius Agrippa and Paracelsus.[43]

Role in the Book: The Mystic Cryptographer. Trithemius authored Polygraphiae (published 1518), the first printed book on cryptography.[44]

Connection to Thesis: Trithemius explicitly linked cryptography to the sacred and the occult. His "Ave Maria" cipher, for example, hid a secret message within the text of a Latin prayer, using each word to stand for a letter.[45] This work formalizes the idea presented in Codex Obscura that encryption was not just for secrecy but for consecration—a ritual act to protect sacred or dangerous knowledge (medical, alchemical) from the uninitiated.

III. The Classical & Medieval Foundations: Authorities in the Deciphered Text

The "Triadic Cipher System" thesis is only valid if the resulting Latin text is meaningful. "Meaningful" in the 15th century meant being in dialogue with the foundational authorities of antiquity. This section proves that the deciphered content—specific remedies, agricultural techniques, and astronomical models—corresponds exactly to the knowledge contained in the core texts of a Quattrocento practitioner's library.

Pedanius Dioscorides (c. 40–90 AD)

Life Story: A Greek physician, pharmacologist, and botanist from Anazarbus, Cilicia, who served as a physician in the Roman army.[46]

Role in the Book: The Foundational Pharmacologist. His five-volume work De Materia Medica ("On Medical Materials") was the single most important pharmacological text in Europe for over 1,500 years, establishing a systematic framework for cataloging substances by their medicinal effects.[47] It was the undisputed, foundational reference for any medieval or Renaissance physician.[48]

Connection to Thesis: Dioscorides' work provides the primary external corroboration for the book's medical decipherments:

- **Folio 6v (Hemorrhoid Remedy):** Codex Obscura deciphers a remedy using teasel (Dipsacos).

This is confirmed by historical sources noting
Dioscorides recommended teasel root for anal
fissures.[49]

- **Folio 66r (Surgical Plaster):** Codex
  Obscura deciphers the term διὰ χυλῶν (diachýlōn), a
  specific plaster made with iris root. This is a technical
  Greek loanword attested in Dioscorides.[50]
- **Folio 6r (Groundsel):** Codex Obscura notes
  Dioscorides described the plant avia (groundsel) and its
  potent properties.[51]
-

Pliny the Elder (Gaius Plinius Secundus) (AD 23/24–79)

Life Story: A Roman author, naturalist, and naval and army
commander of the early Roman Empire.[52] He famously died while
attempting to rescue friends during the eruption of Vesuvius.[53]

Role in the Book: The Encyclopedist of the Natural World.
His Naturalis Historia (Natural History) is the largest single work to
survive from the Roman Empire, a massive encyclopedia of
astronomy, geography, botany, agriculture, pharmacology, and
mineralogy.[54] It was a foundational text for the Renaissance and one
of the first classical works to be printed (Venice, 1469).[55]

Connection to Thesis: Pliny's work, alongside Dioscorides, forms
the basis of the Codex Obscura author's knowledge:

- **Folio 6v (Hemorrhoid Remedy):** Codex
  Obscura cites Pliny for documenting the use of castor
  oil (cici), the second ingredient, for anal inflammation.[56]
- **Folio 4A (Coan Wine):** Codex Obscura cites
  Pliny's Natural History (Book 14) for its specific
  description of vinum Coum and its unique preparation
  with seawater.[57]

- **Folio 33v (Agriculture):** Codex Obscura cites Pliny as a source for the Roman practice of burning farmland (stubble) to improve yields, corroborating the uro ("I burn") decipherment.[58]

Cato the Elder (Marcus Porcius Cato) (234–149 BC)

Life Story: A Roman soldier, senator, consul, and historian known for his rigid morals and defense of Roman traditions.

Role in the Book: The Original Latin Agronomist. His De Agri Cultura ("On Agriculture") is the oldest surviving complete work of Latin prose.[59] It is a practical, if terse, manual for running a farm, with sections on vineyards, slaves, and even medical recipes.[60]

Connection to Thesis: Cato's work plays a direct and critical role in validating the decipherment of the Rosettes foldout. De Agri Cultura contains a specific recipe for making a Coan-style wine (vinum Coum), explicitly detailing the addition of seawater.[61] This provides unimpeachable classical attestation for the exact phrase deciphered in Chapter 5.

Lucius Junius Moderatus Columella (AD 4–c. 70)

Life Story: A Roman writer, born in Hispania Baetica (modern Cádiz, Spain).[62] After a military career as a tribune in Syria, he retired to become a prominent farmer in Italy.[63]

Role in the Book: The Master of Roman Agricultural Science. His 12-book De Re Rustica ("On Agriculture") is the most "comprehensive, systematic and detailed" agricultural treatise from antiquity, easily surpassing his predecessors.[64]

Connection to Thesis: Columella's work was a foundational source for later agronomists, including Pietro de' Crescenzi. His relevance to Codex Obscura (Ch 3, note 10) is his attestation, alongside Pliny, of the practice of burning agricultural land (e.g., stubble) to clear it and control pests, which supports the uro ("I burn") decipherment on Folio 33v.[65]

Pietro de' Crescenzi (c. 1230–c. 1321)

Life Story: A Bolognese jurist who, after retiring from his legal career, wrote a comprehensive treatise on agriculture based on classical sources (like Columella and Cato) and his own practical experience as a landowner.[66]

Role in the Book: The Definitive Quattrocento Agricultural Authority. His Ruralia Commoda (c. 1304-1309) is "considered the most important agricultural treatise of the Middle Ages".[67]

Connection to Thesis: Crescenzi's work was immensely popular in the 15th century, with 15 printed editions in Latin, Italian, French, and German before 1500.[68] This makes it the standard, up-to-date reference for the author of MS 408. Its role in Codex Obscura (Ch 3) is to establish the context for agriculture in 15th-century Lombardy. The sophisticated, intensive, non-fallowing system Crescenzi describes is used to argue against interpreting uro ("I burn") as extensive slash-and-burn, and for the correct interpretation: the controlled burning of stubble on permanent, terraced fields.

Claudius Ptolemy (c. AD 100–c. 170)

Life Story: A Greek mathematician, astronomer, and geographer who lived and worked in Roman Alexandria.[69]

Role in the Book: The Architect of the Pre-Modern Cosmos. Ptolemy's Almagest is "one of the most influential scientific texts in history".[70] It "canonized a geocentric model of the Universe that was accepted for more than 1,200 years".[71]

Connection to Thesis: This model—with a stationary Earth at the center and the heavens rotating on a fixed axis—was the undisputed scientific fact of the 15th century.[72] Codex Obscura's entire analysis of the astronomical folios (Ch 9, 10) is predicated on this Ptolemaic system. The deciphered term cardo ("hinge" or "axis") is the technical Latin term for the celestial pole, the unmoving pivot of the entire Ptolemaic "Celestial Engine."

IV. The Philosophical & Cosmological Framework

The manuscript is not just a practical manual; it is a philosophical one. The deciphered phrases reveal a coherent worldview that integrates science, magic, and theology. This section profiles the thinkers who built that worldview. Boethius provides the central metaphor (the stable cardo of heaven vs. the turning wheel of earth). Denys the Carthusian provides the chronological proof that Boethius was being actively studied at the exact moment the manuscript was created. Ficino provides the operative mechanism (spiritus mundi) that explains how the astronomy functions as iatromathematics.

Anicius Manlius Severinus Boethius (c. 480–524 AD)

Life Story: A Roman senator, consul, and philosopher who sought to translate the entire works of Plato and Aristotle into Latin.[73] He fell from favor, was accused of treason by the Ostrogothic King Theodoric, imprisoned, and unjustly executed.[74]

Role in the Book: The Philosopher of the Cardo. His masterpiece, De Consolatione Philosophiae ("The Consolation of Philosophy"), written in prison, was one of the most widely read and influential books of all time, a foundational text for the Middle Ages and Renaissance.[75]

Connection to Thesis: The Consolation's central argument—delivered by the allegorical Lady Philosophy—is the contrast between the chaotic, unpredictable turnings of Fortune's Wheel (earthly life) and the serene, eternal, rational order of the cosmos, which is governed by divine love and pivots on a fixed axis.[76] This is precisely the philosophy Codex Obscura deciphers from the astronomical folios. The "King" (Rex) at the cardo (pole) is the ultimate Boethian symbol of divine, unmoving reason.

Denys the Carthusian (Dionysius van Rijkel) (1402–1471)

Life Story: A Carthusian monk, prolific theologian, and mystic, Denys was one of the most prolific Latin writers of the Middle Ages.[77] He was renowned for his learning and was consulted by figures across Europe.

Role in the Book: The Contemporary Anchor. Denys's dates (1402–1471) perfectly overlap the radiocarbon dating of the manuscript's vellum (1404–1438).[78]

Connection to Thesis: Denys's critical importance is that he authored a "line-by-line commentary on Boethius' De consolatione philosophiae".[79] This is the scholarly anchor for the Boethian interpretation: it proves that the Consolation was not an ancient, dusty text but was the subject of active, contemporary study and interpretatio christiana (Christian interpretation)[80] at the very moment MS 408 was being written. Denys confirms the Boethian worldview was current in the 1430s.

Marsilio Ficino (1433–1499)

Life Story: A major Italian humanist philosopher and priest, Ficino led the revival of Neoplatonism as the head of the Florentine Platonic Academy, sponsored by Cosimo de' Medici.[81]

Role in the Book: The Architect of Renaissance Natural Magic. His De vita libri tres ("Three Books on Life"), particularly Book 3, De vita coelitus comparanda ("On Obtaining Life from the Heavens," 1489), is the key theoretical text for the manuscript's worldview.[82]

Connection to Thesis: Ficino argued that a universal spiritus mundi ("World-Soul") animates the cosmos, acting as a medium that transmits the influentia (virtues) of the stars and planets to the corresponding spiritus in man.[83] This spiritus could be attracted and captured through sympathetic materials—herbs, gems, colors—and focused intentio (will). This is the exact philosophical and magical engine behind Codex Obscura's "Ladle Invocation." It explains why the author would use astronomical diagrams: not just for observation, but for iatromathematics—the operative timing of rituals to imbue remedies with celestial power.

Paracelsus (Theophrastus von Hohenheim) (1493–1541)

Life Story: A Swiss physician, alchemist, and reformer of medicine, known for his combustible personality and his rejection of traditional Galenic humorism. He was a student of Johannes Trithemius.[84]

Role in the Book: The Toxicological Benchmark. Paracelsus is mentioned in Codex Obscura (Ch 5, Ch 8) as a post-facto articulator of a principle the manuscript's author already understood: "sola dosis facit venenum" ("only the dose makes the poison").[85]

Connection to Thesis: The decipherment of Folio 6r, which details the harvesting of a potent "singular sap" (oenus lac) from the toxic groundsel plant (avia), demonstrates a sophisticated, pre-Paracelsian understanding of toxicology. Paracelsus serves as a historical marker to show that the manuscript's author was an experimental pharmacologist working at the cutting edge of 15th-century science.

V. Contextual Figures & The Counter-Theories

To establish the "ciphered Latin" thesis as definitive, one must dismantle the major counter-theories. This section profiles the proponents of those theories, providing the scholarly context for the "Objections & Replies" appendix. Each major counter-theory is a product of its creator's own specialized expertise (computing, cryptography, botany, respectively). Their inability to solve the codex stems from a lack of the interdisciplinary approach (cryptography + philology + art history + pharmacology) that the Codex Obscura thesis provides.

Roger Bacon (c. 1219/20–c. 1292)

Life Story: A 13th-century English philosopher, Franciscan friar, and Doctor Mirabilis ("Wondrous Doctor") who advocated for empirical methods and wrote on alchemy and ciphers.[86]

Role in the Book: The Legendary (but Incorrect) Author. Bacon is central to the manuscript's mythology. Marci's 1665 letter mentions the rumor of his authorship, which was eagerly adopted by Wilfrid Voynich.[87]

Connection to Thesis: Bacon's reputation made him a compelling medieval candidate. The Codex Obscura thesis, however, relies on the definitive 15th-century radiocarbon dating (1404–1438) to refute this attribution.[88] Bacon is important because he represents the "lost medieval wisdom" narrative that has obscured the manuscript's true Quattrocento Italian origins.

William F. Friedman (1891–1969)

Life Story: Born Wolf Friedman in Russia, he became one of America's greatest cryptographers.[89] He ran the Army's Signal Intelligence Service and led the team that broke Japan's "PURPLE" diplomatic cipher before World War II.[90]

Role in the Book: Proponent of the "Artificial Language" Theory. Friedman is the most formidable authority to have tackled the manuscript. After his "First Study Group" of Army cryptanalysts (1944–46) failed to break the text,[91] he concluded that its highly regular, repetitive structure was not a cipher of a natural language.

Connection to Thesis: Friedman famously theorized it was a constructed, a priori philosophical language.[92] Codex Obscura directly refutes this. It argues that the "artificial" properties (like word regularity) are not from the language but are artifacts of the cipher itself—specifically, the "Triadic Cipher System's" systematic use of nulls and permutation commands.

Gordon Rugg

Life Story: A contemporary British academic specializing in computing and psychology at Keele University.

Role in the Book: Proponent of the "Elegant Hoax" Theory. In 2004, Rugg argued the text is meaningless "gibberish".[93] He demonstrated that a 16th-century cryptographic tool, the Cardan grille, used with tables of syllables, could procedurally generate text that mimics the manuscript's statistical properties.[94]

Connection to Thesis: Codex Obscura refutes this popular theory on two primary, non-negotiable grounds:

1. **Anachronism:** The Cardan grille (c. 1550)[95] did not exist when the manuscript's vellum was prepared (1404–1438).[96]
2. **Semantic Content:** The hoax model is incapable of producing the deep, verifiable, and consistent text-image coherence that the "Triadic Cipher System" reveals (e.g., the διὰ χυλῶν (diachýlon) recipe on the surgery folio, the Dorio toponym on the cardoon folio).

Arthur O. Tucker and Jules Janick

Life Story: Contemporary American botanists and professors of horticulture at Delaware State University and Purdue University, respectively.[97]

Role in the Book: Proponents of the "Mesoamerican (Aztec) Origin" Theory. Their theory is based entirely on iconographic interpretation from their field of expertise: botany. They argue the manuscript is a 16th-century Mexican codex,[98] identifying numerous plants (like the sunflower) and animals (like the armadillo) as New World species.[99]

Connection to Thesis: Codex Obscura refutes this theory as materially and historically impossible, citing:

1. **Anachronism:** The radiocarbon date (1404–1438) makes a post-1492, 16th-century New World origin impossible.[100]
2. **European Iconography:** The theory fails to account for the unambiguously European content, such as the classical zodiac and, most importantly, the Ghibelline swallowtail merlons on the castle of Ameria.
3. **Linguistic Evidence:** The theory has failed to produce any verifiable Nahuatl decipherment,[101] whereas the Codex Obscura thesis provides verifiable Italian toponyms ("Dorio," "Ameria") in ciphered Latin.

Notes

1. "Rudolf II, Holy Roman Emperor," Wikipedia, last modified October 2025.
2. Raymond Clemens, ed., The Voynich Manuscript (New Haven: Yale University Press, 2016).

156

3. René Zandbergen, "Earliest Owners," in The Voynich Manuscript, ed. Raymond Clemens (New Haven: Yale University Press, 2016).

4. "Athanasius Kircher," Wikipedia, last modified October 2025 ; Daniel K. Stolzenberg, "Athanasius Kircher," The Eye of the Lynx (University of Chicago Press, 2018).

5. "Rudolf II, Holy Roman Emperor".

6. "Rudolf II, Holy Roman Emperor".

7. "Rudolf II, Holy Roman Emperor".

8. "Cabinets of curiosities and the Wunderkammer of Rudolf II in Prague," Europeana, accessed October 29, 2025.

9. "Cabinets of curiosities and the Wunderkammer of Rudolf II in Prague".

10. Zandbergen, "Earliest Owners" ; René Zandbergen, "The history of the Voynich MS," voynich.nu, accessed October 29, 2025.

11. Clemens, The Voynich Manuscript.

12. Zandbergen, "The history of the Voynich MS".

13. Clemens, The Voynich Manuscript.

14. Zandbergen, "Earliest Owners".

15. Zandbergen, "The history of the Voynich MS".

16. Zandbergen, "Earliest Owners" ; James Trilling, "The Voynich Manuscript," Journal of the History of Ideas (2021) ; René Zandbergen, "The 1665 letter of J.M. Marci," voynich.nu, accessed October 29, 2025.

17. Zandbergen, "The 1665 letter of J.M. Marci" ; Zandbergen, "The history of the Voynich MS".

18. Clemens, The Voynich Manuscript ; Zandbergen, "Earliest Owners" ; Trilling, "The Voynich Manuscript".

19. "Athanasius Kircher," Wikipedia ; "Athanasius Kircher," Internet Encyclopedia of Philosophy ; Stolzenberg, "Athanasius Kircher".

20. "Athanasius Kircher," Wikipedia ; "Athanasius Kircher," IEP.

21. "Athanasius Kircher," IEP.

22. Trilling, "The Voynich Manuscript" ; "Athanasius Kircher," Wikipedia.

23. Zandbergen, "Earliest Owners".

24. "Wilfrid Voynich," Wikipedia, last modified October 2025.

25. "Wilfrid Voynich," Wikipedia.

26. Zandbergen, "Earliest Owners" ; "Wilfrid Voynich," Wikipedia.

27. "Wilfrid (Michał) Wojnicz, an emigrant antiquarian," Kuryer Polski, accessed October 29, 2025.

28. Augusto Buonafalce, "Cicco Simonetta's Cipher-Breaking Rules," Cryptologia 32, no. 1 (2008) ; Nick Pelling, "Fifteenth Century Cryptography," Cipher Mysteries (blog), July 6, 2016.

29. Xintong Yang, "Not Disk but System: The Meaning of 'formula' in Alberti's De Cifris," Advances in History Studies (2023) ; "Alberti's 'La Cifra'," Carnegie Mellon University Libraries, accessed October 29, 2025.

30. "Federico da Montefeltro Duke of Urbino," The History Blog, accessed October 29, 2025 ; Antoine M. Wilmering, "The Liberal Arts Studiolo from the Ducal Palace at Gubbio," The Metropolitan Museum of Art Bulletin 53, no. 4 (Spring 1996).

31. Yang, "Not Disk but System".

32. "Alberti's 'La Cifra'".

33. "Alberti's 'La Cifra'".

34. Yang, "Not Disk but System" ; "Can you break this encryption invented in 1467?" Medium, accessed October 29, 2025.

35. "Alberti's 'La Cifra'".

36. Buonafalce, "Cicco Simonetta's Cipher-Breaking Rules".

37. Buonafalce, "Cicco Simonetta's Cipher-Breaking Rules".

38. Nick Pelling, "Fifteenth Century Cryptography Revisited," (Draft paper, 2017).

39. "Federico da Montefeltro," Wikipedia, last modified October 2025.

40. Wilmering, "The Liberal Arts Studiolo" ; "Federico da Montefeltro Duke of Urbino," The History Blog.

41. "Federico da Montefeltro Duke of Urbino," The History Blog.

42. "Johannes Trithemius," Wikipedia, last modified October 2025 ; "Johannes Trithemius," Books of Magick, accessed October 29, 2025.

43. "Johannes Trithemius," Wikipedia.

44. "Johannes Trithemius Issues the First Book on Cryptography," History of Information, accessed October 29, 2025 ; "Polygraphia (book)," Wikipedia, last modified October 2025 ; "Polygraphiae libri sex," Archive.org.

45. "Johannes Trithemius Issues the First Book on Cryptography" ; "Polygraphia (book)".

46. "Pedanius Dioscorides," EBSCO Research Starters, accessed October 29, 2025 ; "De materia medica," Wikipedia, last modified October 2025.

47. "De materia medica" ; John M. Riddle, "Dioscorides's De materia medica..." Journal of Ethnopharmacology (2010) ; John M. Riddle, Review of De Materia Medica by Pedanius Dioscorides, trans. Lily Y. Beck, Journal of the History of Medicine and Allied Sciences 61.2 (2006).

48. Riddle, Review of De Materia Medica ; "Pedanius Dioscorides," EBSCO.

49. Pedanius Dioscorides, De Materia Medica.

50. Pedanius Dioscorides, De Materia Medica.

51. Pedanius Dioscorides, De Materia Medica, Book IV, Chapter 96.

52. "Natural History (Pliny)," Wikipedia, last modified October 2025 ; Stuart, "Studies in the Career of Pliny the Elder..." (PhD diss., St. Andrews, 1996).

53. Stuart, "Studies in the Career of Pliny the Elder".

54. "Natural History (Pliny)".

55. "Natural History (Pliny)" ; Marco V. Garcia, "Pliny the Elder's Natural History," Umanistica Digitale (2020).

56. Pliny the Elder, Naturalis Historia, 23.83.

57. Pliny the Elder, Naturalis Historia, 14.78.

58. Pliny the Elder, Naturalis Historia.

59. "De agri cultura," Encyclopaedia Romana, accessed October 29, 2025.

60. "De agri cultura," Wikipedia, last modified October 2025., "Cato's De Agri Cultura and the Roman Agricultural Economy," Journal of Roman Studies (2020).

61. Marcus Cato, De Agri Cultura, trans. W. D. Hooper (Loeb Classical Library, 1934) ; "Recipe for Coan wine," Loeb Classical Library.

62. "Lucius Junius Moderatus Columella," Wikipedia, last modified October 2025 ; Roman Agronomic Knowledge Of Viticulture Through Lucius Columella (2022) ; "Lucius Junius Moderatus Columella," Archive.org.

63. "Lucius Junius Moderatus Columella," Encyclopaedia Britannica, accessed October 29, 2025 ; "Lucius Junius Moderatus Columella," Wikipedia.

64. "Columella," Loeb Classical Library, accessed October 29, 2025 ; "Columella," Oxford Bibliographies, accessed October 29, 2025.
65. Columella, De Re Rustica.
66. "Pietro Crescenzi," History of Information, accessed October 29, 2025 ; "Pietro de' Crescenzi," Harvard University Herbaria, accessed October 29, 2025 ; "Petrus de Crescentius, Ruralia commoda, 1471," University of Reading, accessed October 29, 2025.
67. "Petrus de Crescentius, Ruralia commoda," Royal Collection Trust, accessed October 29, 2025 ; "Petrus de Crescentius, Ruralia commoda, 1471," University of Reading.
68. "Pietro Crescenzi," History of Information ; "Petrus de Crescentius, Ruralia commoda," Royal Collection Trust.
69. Mirjana Uzelac, "Claudius Ptolemy & His Geocentric Model of the Universe," The Collector, December 10, 2023 ; "The Legacy of Ptolemy's Almagest," American Institute of Physics, accessed October 29, 2025.
70. "Almagest," Wikipedia, last modified October 2025 ; Olaf Pedersen, "A Survey of the Almagest," (Springer, 2011).
71. "Almagest," Wikipedia ; Uzelac, "Claudius Ptolemy".
72. "The Legacy of Ptolemy's Almagest" ; "The Legacy of Ptolemy's Almagest," American Institute of Physics, October 11, 2022.
73. "Boethius," Internet Encyclopedia of Philosophy, accessed October 29, 2025.
74. Editorial Note, The Consolation of Philosophy (Ex-Classics, 2009) ; Erica Weaver and A. Joseph McMullen, "Reading Boethius in Medieval England," eScholarship (2018).
75. Editorial Note, The Consolation of Philosophy ; Lodi Nauta, "The Popularity of Boethius's Consolatio," International Journal of the Classical Tradition (2009) ; Weaver and McMullen, "Reading Boethius".
76. Editorial Note, The Consolation of Philosophy ; Weaver and McMullen, "Reading Boethius".
77. Kent Emery, Jr., "A complete reception of the Latin Corpus Dionysiacum," Analecta Cartusiana (1990).
78. Emery, Jr., "A complete reception".

79. Nauta, "The Popularity of Boethius's Consolatio" ; Emery, Jr., "A complete reception" ; R. Macken, Denys the Carthusian: Commentator on Boethius's De consolatione philosophiae.
80. Reinhold F. Glei, et al., eds., Boethius christianus? Transformationen der "consolatio Philosophiae" (Berlin, 2010).
81. "Marsilio Ficino," Stanford Encyclopedia of Philosophy, last modified October 2022.
82. "Marsilio Ficino, De vita libri tres," PRPH Books, accessed October 29, 2025 ; Denis J.-J. Robichaud, "Ficino on Force, Magic, and Prayers," Renaissance Quarterly 70, no. 1 (Spring 2017).
83. Marsilio Ficino, De vita coelitus comparanda.
84. "Johannes Trithemius," Wikipedia.
85. Paracelsus, Septem Defensiones (1538).
86. Clemens, The Voynich Manuscript.
87. Clemens, The Voynich Manuscript ; Zandbergen, "Earliest Owners" ; "Wilfrid (Michał) Wojnicz".
88. "Voynich manuscript," Wikipedia, last modified October 2025 ; Trilling, "The Voynich Manuscript".
89. "William F. Friedman," voynich.nu, accessed October 29, 2025.
90. "William F. Friedman," Wikipedia, last modified October 2025.
91. "William F. Friedman," voynich.nu ; Jim Reeds, "William F. Friedman," (1994).
92. "William F. Friedman," voynich.nu ; Reeds, "William F. Friedman".
93. René Zandbergen, "The Cardan grille approach to the Voynich MS taken to the next level," arXiv (2021) ; Nick Pelling, "Gordon Rugg, the man who cracked the mystery of the Voynich Manuscript? Cracks... not," Cipher Mysteries (blog), September 14, 2016 ; "Gordon Rugg," voynich.ninja, accessed October 29, 2025.
94. Zandbergen, "The Cardan grille approach" ; Pelling, "Gordon Rugg".
95. Zandbergen, "The Cardan grille approach".
96. Gordon Rugg, "An Elegant Hoax? A Possible Solution to the Voynich Manuscript," Cryptologia 28, no. 1 (2004).
97. "Purdue and Delaware State professors unravel century-old mystery," Purdue University News, (2018) ; "Purdue horticulture professor earns award," Purdue University News, (2020).

98. "Purdue and Delaware State professors" ; Arthur O. Tucker and Jules Janick, Unraveling the Voynich Codex (Cham: Springer, 2018) ; "Was the Voynich Manuscript Written in Nahuatl?" Nahuatl Studies (blog), (2018) ; "The Voynich Manuscript: Aztec Herbal from New Spain," ResearchGate.

99. "Purdue and Delaware State professors" ; "Purdue horticulture professor earns award".

100. "Purdue and Delaware State professors".

101. Tucker and Janick, Unraveling the Voynich Codex ; Matthew Nicholson, Review of Unraveling the Voynich Codex, The Botanical Gardener (2023).

WORKS CITED

Rudolf II, Holy Roman Emperor - Wikipedia, https://en.wikipedia.org/wiki/Rudolf_II,_Holy_Roman_Emperor https://scholarworks.iu.edu/journals/index.php/tmr/article/download/23836/29526

Mysterious Voynich Manuscript reborn in facsimile edition | Yale News, https://news.yale.edu/2016/10/31/mysterious-voynich-manuscript-reborn-facsimile-edition

Athanasius Kircher - Wikipedia, https://en.wikipedia.org/wiki/Athanasius_Kircher

Father Kircher's Big Beautiful Books in - Brill, https://brill.com/view/journals/jjs/9/1/article-p137_137.xml?language=en

Cabinets of curiosities and the Wunderkammer of Rudolf II in Prague | Europeana, https://www.europeana.eu/en/stories/cabinets-of-curiosities-and-the-wunderkammer-of-rudolf-ii-in-prague

The history of the Voynich MS, https://www.voynich.nu/history.html

THE UNKNOWN IS STILL WINNING: THE VOYNICH MANUSCRIPT - Project MUSE, https://muse.jhu.edu/article/792400/summary

17th Century letters related to the MS - Voynich.nu, https://www.voynich.nu/letters.html

Athanasius Kircher | Research Starters - EBSCO, https://www.ebsco.com/research-starters/religion-and-philosophy/athanasius-kircher

Wilfrid Voynich - Wikipedia, https://en.wikipedia.org/wiki/Wilfrid_Voynich

Wilfrid Voynich – a Polish Antiquarian Who Found a Mysterious Manuscript - Kuryer Polski, https://kuryerpolski.us/en/Page/View/michal-wojnicz

The Professionalization of Cryptology in Sixteenth-Century Venice | Enterprise & Society, https://www.cambridge.org/core/journals/enterprise-and-society/article/professionalization-of-cryptology-in-sixteenthcentury-venice/4C1A7D44C76A4CD7F421A27D1CBDD4D5

Fifteenth century cryptography... - Cipher Mysteries, https://ciphermysteries.com/2016/07/06/fifteenth-century-cryptography

Not Disk but System: The Meaning of "formula" in Alberti's De Cifris, https://madison-proceedings.com/index.php/aehssr/article/download/1606/1600/3327

New to CMU Libraries' Special Collections: The First Western Treatise on Cryptography & Mechanical Encryption, https://www.library.cmu.edu/about/news/2023-01/Alberti-La-Cifra

The Duke of Urbino's magical studiolo - The History Blog, https://www.thehistoryblog.com/archives/63879

The Liberal Arts Studiolo from the Ducal Palace at Gubbio: The Metropolitan Museum of Art Bulletin, v. 53, no. 4 (Spring, 1996), https://resources.metmuseum.org/resources/metpublications/pdf/The_Liberal_Arts_Studiolo_from_the_Ducal_Palace_at_Gubbio_The_Metropolitan_Museum_of_Art_Bulletin_v_53_no_4_Spring_1996.pdf?_gl=1*jee801*_ga*MjIyMjEzNzE0LjE3MDQ4OTg2Mzg.*_ga_Y0W8DGNBTB*MTcwNTMyNzY1NC4yLjEuMTcwNTMyNzY2NC4wLjAuMA..

Can You Break This Encryption Invented In 1467? | by S.W. Bowen | Cantor's Paradise, https://www.cantorsparadise.com/can-you-break-this-encryption-invented-in-1467-c13c324afde1

New paper on fifteenth century cryptography - Cipher Mysteries, https://ciphermysteries.com/2017/07/08/new-paper-fifteenth-century-cryptography

Federico da Montefeltro - Wikipedia, https://en.wikipedia.org/wiki/Federico_da_Montefeltro

Johannes Trithemius - Wikipedia, https://en.wikipedia.org/wiki/Johannes_Trithemius

Polygraphie et universelle escriture cabalistique - Grimoire Magic, https://booksofmagick.com/polygraphiae/

Johannes Trithemius Issues the First Book on Cryptography - History of Information, https://www.historyofinformation.com/detail.php?id=348

Polygraphia (book) - Wikipedia, https://en.wikipedia.org/wiki/Polygraphia_(book)

Polygraphie et vniuerselle escriture cabalistique : Trithemius, Johannes, 1462-1516 : Free Download, Borrow, and Streaming - Internet Archive, https://archive.org/details/polygraphieetvni00trit

Pedanius Dioscorides | Research Starters - EBSCO, https://www.ebsco.com/research-starters/biography/pedanius-dioscorides

De materia medica - Wikipedia, https://en.wikipedia.org/wiki/De_materia_medica

European Materia Medica in Historical Texts: Longevity of a Tradition and Implications for Future Use - NIH, https://pmc.ncbi.nlm.nih.gov/articles/PMC2956839/

De materia medica by Pedanius Dioscorides (review) - ResearchGate, https://www.researchgate.net/publication/265746644_De_materia_medica_by_Pedanius_Dioscorides_review

Natural History (Pliny) - Wikipedia, https://en.wikipedia.org/wiki/Natural_History_(Pliny)

Pliny's defense of empire - LSU Scholarly Repository, https://repository.lsu.edu/cgi/viewcontent.cgi?article=4313&context=gradschool_dissertations

View of Modeling the Sources and Topics of Pliny's Natural History | Umanistica Digitale, https://umanisticadigitale.unibo.it/article/view/12521/13778

Wine and Rome, https://penelope.uchicago.edu/encyclopaedia_romana/wine/wine.html

De agri cultura - Wikipedia, https://en.wikipedia.org/wiki/De_agri_cultura

Cato the Elder on Human and Animal Diseases and Medicines for Them – According to the Treatise on "Agriculture" | Classica Cracoviensia - Academic Journals of Księgarnia Akademicka Publishing, https://journals.akademicka.pl/cc/article/view/885

LacusCurtius • Cato On Agriculture — Sections 104-125, https://penelope.uchicago.edu/Thayer/e/roman/texts/cato/de_agricultura/g*.html

Delphi Complete Works of Cato the Elder (Illustrated), https://ia600705.us.archive.org/35/items/cato-on-agriculture/Cato%20on%20Agriculture%20%28Berserker%20Books%29.pdf

Columella - Wikipedia, https://en.wikipedia.org/wiki/Columella

roman agronomic knowledge of viticulture through lucius columella and his uncle marcus in hispania - ResearchGate, https://www.researchgate.net/publication/370516716_ROM AN_AGRONOMIC_KNOWLEDGE_OF_VITICULTUR E_THROUGH_LUCIUS_COLUMELLA_AND_HIS_UN CLE_MARCUS_IN_HISPANIA/download

lucius junius - moderatus columella - on agriculture, https://ia601502.us.archive.org/13/items/in.ernet.dli.2015.4 81324/2015.481324.losang-gongyen_text.pdf

Lucius Junius Moderatus Columella | Agriculturalist, Naturalist, Writer - Britannica, https://www.britannica.com/biography/Lucius-Junius-Moderatus-Columella

Columella, On Agriculture, Volume I: Books 1-4 | Loeb Classical Library, https://www.loebclassics.com/view/LCL361/1941/volume. xml

Columella - Classics - Oxford Bibliographies, https://www.oxfordbibliographies.com/abstract/document/ obo-9780195389661/obo-9780195389661-0203.xml

Crescentius's Ruralia Commoda: Agriculture, Animal Husbandry, and Horticulture, https://www.historyofinformation.com/detail.php?id=2223

Pietro Crescenzi | Harvard University Herbaria & Libraries, https://www.huh.harvard.edu/book/pietro-crescenzi

Petrus de Crescentius, Ruralia commoda, 1471 - Museums and Collections – University of Reading, https://collections.reading.ac.uk/special-collections/wp-content/uploads/sites/5/2020/01/Featured-Item_Crescentius-Ruralia-commoda-1471.pdf

Pietro de' Crescenzi (c. 1233-c. 1320) - Ruralia Commoda - Royal Collection Trust, https://www.rct.uk/collection/1057436/ruralia-commoda

Get to Know Claudius Ptolemy & His Geocentric Model of the Universe | TheCollector, https://www.thecollector.com/claudius-ptolemy-geocentric-model-universe/

Initial Conditions Episode 11: The Legacy of Ptolemy's Almagest - AIP.ORG, https://www.aip.org/library/initial-conditions-episode-11-the-legacy-of-ptolemys-almagest-1742381776081

Almagest - Wikipedia, https://en.wikipedia.org/wiki/Almagest

A Survey of the Almagest - ResearchGate, https://www.researchgate.net/publication/234344396_A_Su rvey_of_the_Almagest

Boethius | Internet Encyclopedia of Philosophy, https://iep.utm.edu/boethius/

The Consolation of Philosophy Anicius Manlius Severinus Boethius - Ex-Classics, https://www.exclassics.com/consol/consol.pdf

The Legacy of Boethius in Medieval England: The Consolation and its Afterlives - eScholarship, https://escholarship.org/content/qt907252xd/qt907252xd_ noSplash_6164553d0d40fa25e1554de7de72531e.pdf

A Humanist Reading of Boethius's Consolatio Philosophiae: The Commentary by Murmellius and Agricola (1514)* Lodi Nauta 1. The Co, https://www.rug.nl/staff/l.w.nauta/murmellius.pdf

A COMPLETE RECEPTION OF THE LATIN CORPUS DIONYSIACUM: THE COMMENTARIES OF DENYS THE CARTHUSIAN In this essay, I shall discuss (I - CARTUSIANA, http://www.cartusiana.org/sites/default/files/Emery_A%20 complete%20reception%20of%20the%20Latin%20Corpus% 20Dionysiacum.pdf

BOETHIUS: FIRST OF THE SCHOLASTICS* - University of Toronto, http://individual.utoronto.ca/pking/articles/boethius_on_consolation.pdf

BOETHIUS'S INFLUENCE ON GERMAN LITERATURE TO c.1500 Christine Hehle The German-language reception of Boethius does not form a - Brill, https://brill.com/downloadpdf/book/edcoll/978900422538 1/B9789004225381_009.pdf

Marsilio Ficino - Stanford Encyclopedia of Philosophy, https://plato.stanford.edu/entries/ficino

Marsilio Ficino, Astrology, and Renaissance Magic - PRPH Books, https://www.prphbooks.com/blog/ficino-astrology-magic

Ficino on Force, Magic, and Prayers: Neoplatonic and Hermetic Influences in Ficino's Three Books on Life | Renaissance Quarterly | Cambridge Core, https://www.cambridge.org/core/journals/renaissance-quarterly/article/ficino-on-force-magic-and-prayers-neoplatonic-and-hermetic-influences-in-ficinos-three-books-on-life/D58BF87BF014749B95F2FC06F7120941

Voynich manuscript - Wikipedia, https://en.wikipedia.org/wiki/Voynich_manuscript

History of research of the Voynich MS, https://www.voynich.nu/solvers.html

William F. Friedman - Wikipedia, https://en.wikipedia.org/wiki/William_F._Friedman

William F. Friedman's Transcription of the Voynich Manuscript - Apprendre-en-ligne.net, https://www.apprendre-en-ligne.net/crypto/mystere/wff.pdf

The Cardan grille approach to the Voynich MS taken to the ... - arXiv, https://arxiv.org/abs/2104.12548

Gordon Rugg, "The Man Who Cracked The Mystery Of The Voynich Manuscript", cracks it once again (NOT), https://ciphermysteries.com/2016/09/14/gordon-rugg-man-cracked-mystery-voynich-manuscript-cracks-not

The Cardan grille approach to the Voynich MS taken to the next level, https://www.voynich.ninja/thread-3537.html

An Elegant Hoax? A Possible Solution to the Voynich Manuscript - ResearchGate, https://www.researchgate.net/publication/233458814_An_Elegant_Hoax_A_Possible_Solution_to_the_Voynich_Manuscript

Purdue and Delaware State professors unravel century-old mystery, https://www.purdue.edu/newsroom/archive/releases/2018/Q3/purdue-and-delaware-state-professors-unravel-century-old-mystery.html

Purdue horticulture professor earns award for illuminating secrets of the Voynich manuscript, https://www.purdue.edu/newsroom/archive/releases/2020/Q1/purdue-horticulture-professor-earns-award-for-illuminating-secrets-of-the-voynich-manuscript.html

Jules Janick Arthur O. Tucker - eBooks, https://content.e-bookshelf.de/media/reading/L-11609003-838bdd51a8.pdf

Unraveling the Voynich Codex | Request PDF - ResearchGate, https://www.researchgate.net/publication/345598891_Unraveling_the_Voynich_Codex

Was the Voynich manuscript written in Nahuatl? - Nawatl Scholar, http://nahuatlstudies.blogspot.com/2018/12/was-voynich-manuscript-written-in.html

(PDF) The Voynich Manuscript: Aztec Herbal from New Spain. - ResearchGate, https://www.researchgate.net/publication/260983778_The_Voynich_Manuscript_Aztec_Herbal_from_New_Spain

174

Unraveling the Voynich Codex by Jules Janick and Arthur O Tucker - Issuu, https://issuu.com/bganz/docs/tbg_iss60_jun2023_final_23 0703/s/27550485

☙

LIST OF ILLUSTRATIONS & CREDITS

Frontispiece. This plain vellum cover of Beinecke MS 408 (the Voynich Manuscript) is preserved at Yale University's Beinecke Library. Its unadorned exterior gives no hint of the cryptographic and botanical mysteries contained inside, underscoring how a modest physical artifact can conceal centuries-old secrets. Unknown author. Cover of the Voynich Manuscript (Beinecke MS 408). Early fifteenth century (manuscript), vellum binding (likely eighteenth century). Beinecke Rare Book & Manuscript Library, Yale University, New Haven, CT, MS 408. https://collections.library.yale.edu/iiif/2/1006074/full/2931,/0/default.jpg.

Figure 1. *Johannes Marcus Marci* (1595–1667), rector of Charles University. This portrait introduces a key historical figure in the manuscript's provenance. Marci's 1665 letter to Athanasius Kircher is the primary source linking the codex to the court of Emperor Rudolf II, grounding the mystery in a specific seventeenthth-century intellectual context. Groos, Gerard de. Joannes Marcus Marci. Line engraving, c. 1650–1700. https://commons.wikimedia.org/wiki/File:Jan_Marcus_Marci_00.jpg.

Figure 2. Marci's 1665 letter to Athanasius Kircher. This is the single most important document for the manuscript's early history. Found inside the codex by Wilfrid Voynich, the letter provides the narrative of ownership by Rudolf II and the belief that it was the work of Roger Bacon, establishing the starting point for all modern research into the manuscript's provenance. Marci, Johannes Marcus. Letter to Athanasius Kircher. August 1665 or 1666. Beinecke Rare Book & Manuscript Library, Yale University, New Haven, CT, MS 408. https://collections.library.yale.edu/iiif/2/1170955/full/full/0/default.jpg.

Figure 3. *Emperor Rudolf II* (1552–1612). The portrait of Emperor Rudolf II establishes the cultural milieu of the manuscript's first known high-profile owner. Rudolf's court in Prague was a center for alchemy, astrology, and the collection of curiosities, explaining why a mysterious, unreadable book would be of immense value and framing it as an object of esoteric knowledge. Sadeler, Aegidius, II. Rudolf II, Holy Roman Emperor. 1603. Engraving. The Elisha Whittelsey Collection, The Elisha Whittelsey Fund, 1951. https://commons.wikimedia.org/wiki/File:Portrait_of_Rudolph_II_MET_DP102234~1.jpg.

Figure 4. Michał Wojnicz (Wilfrid Voynich, 1865–1930). This photograph introduces the manuscript's modern rediscoverer and namesake. Voynich's acquisition of the codex in 1912 marks the beginning of the modern era of its study, personifying its transition from a forgotten relic into a twentieth-century cryptographic obsession. Unknown author. Wilfrid Voynich. Photograph, c. 1920. Wikimedia Commons. https://commons.wikimedia.org/wiki/File:Micha%C5%82_Wojnicz_c._1885.png.

Figure 5. Villa Mondragone near Rome. This image shows the location where Wilfrid Voynich rediscovered the manuscript in 1912, purchasing it from the archives of a Jesuit college. It serves as a geographical anchor for the modern history of the codex, marking the place where it re-emerged into public awareness. Villa Mondragone. Postcard, early 1900s. Wikimedia Commons. https://commons.wikimedia.org/wiki/File:Villa_mondragone_view.jpg.

Figure 6. *Athanasius Kircher* (1602–1680), Jesuit polymath. This portrait depicts the seventeenth-century scholar to whom the manuscript was sent for decipherment. Kircher, a celebrated would-be decoder of Egyptian hieroglyphs, represents the long history of failed attempts to unlock the manuscript's secrets, highlighting the difficulty of the cryptographic challenge. Unknown author. *Athanasius Kircher*. Engraving, seventeenth century. Wikimedia Commons. https://commons.wikimedia.org/w/index.php?curid=442392

Figure 7. Typical Voynich herbal folio. An example from the manuscript's largest section, this image shows a full-page illustration of an unknown or composite plant, surrounded by the unreadable script. It exemplifies the core puzzle of the herbal chapters: the relationship between the unique botanical drawings and the accompanying text. *The Voynich Manuscript* (MS 408), f. 90r. Early fifteenth century. Ink and tempera on vellum. Beinecke Rare Book & Manuscript Library, Yale University, New Haven, CT. https://collections.library.yale.edu/catalog/2002046?child_oid=1006 236.

Figure 8. Voynich astronomical folio. This image, showing celestial bodies arranged in complex circular diagrams, represents the astronomical and astrological content of the manuscript. It illustrates the author's engagement with cosmology and the challenge of interpreting these diagrams, which blend observational astronomy with symbolic imagery. *The Voynich Manuscript* (MS 408), f. 68r. Early fifteenth century. Ink and tempera on vellum. Beinecke Rare Book & Manuscript Library, Yale University, New Haven, CT. https://collections.library.yale.edu/catalog/2002046?child_oid=1006 196.

Figure 9. Voynich "balneological" folio. Representative of the manuscript's most enigmatic section, this folio depicts nude female figures interacting with elaborate, plumbing-like structures filled with green fluid. This imagery has defied easy interpretation and highlights the deeply unconventional and symbolic nature of the codex. *The Voynich Manuscript* (MS 408), f. 78r. Early fifteenth century. Ink and tempera on vellum. Beinecke Rare Book & Manuscript Library, Yale University, New Haven, CT. https://collections.library.yale.edu/catalog/2002046?child_oid=1006 214.

Figure 10. Voynich "recipes" section. This image shows the dense, continuous text that characterizes the final section of the manuscript. The text is marked by star-like symbols in the margins, suggesting a collection of formulas, recipes, or short entries, and represents the challenge of deciphering long passages of pure script without illustrative aids. *The Voynich Manuscript* (MS 408), f. 107r (detail). Early fifteenth century. Ink on vellum. Beinecke Rare Book & Manuscript

Library, Yale University, New Haven, CT. Detail from photograph by Tomhannen. Wikimedia Commons. https://commons.wikimedia.org/wiki/File:Voynich_manuscript_reci pe_example_107r_crop.jpg.

Figure 11. Alberti's cipher disk (c. 1467). This diagram of Leon Battista Alberti's invention, the first polyalphabetic cipher device, serves as a crucial piece of contextual evidence. It demonstrates that sophisticated cryptographic technology was being developed in fifteenth-century Italy, making the complex "Triadic Cipher System" proposed in the book historically plausible. Unknown author. Diagram of an Alberti Cipher Disk. Modern illustration based on fifteenth-century descriptions. Wikimedia Commons. https://commons.wikimedia.org/w/index.php?search=cipher+disk &title=Special%3AMediaSearch&type=image.

Figure 12. *Leon Battista Alberti* (c. 1404–1472), engraved portrait. This portrait of the Renaissance humanist, architect, and cryptographer Leon Battista Alberti visually reinforces his role as a key intellectual figure of the era. His work in cryptography provides the historical and technological context for the book's claims about the Voynich cipher's origins. Kohl, Clemens (after). Alberti, Leon Battista. Engraving, eighteenth century. PICRYL. https://commons.wikimedia.org/wiki/File:Leon_Battista_Alberti2.jp g.

Figure 13. *Leon Battista Alberti* (c. 1404–1472), portrait by Cristofano dell'Altissimo. This painted portrait further establishes the identity of Alberti, whose treatise De Cifris is a cornerstone of Renaissance cryptography and a key piece of evidence for the intellectual environment that could have produced the Voynich Manuscript. Altissimo, Cristofano dell. Leone Batista Alberti. Oil on panel, c. 1588. Uffizi Gallery, Florence. Photograph via Wikimedia Commons. https://commons.wikimedia.org/wiki/File:Leon_Battista_Alberti,_d i_Cristofano_dell%27Altissimo,_1588_-FG.jpg.

Figure 14. Medieval farmer guiding a plow team. This illustration of typical medieval hillside agriculture provides visual context for the decipherment of folio 33v. It grounds the decoded text about cultivating cardoons on sloped land in the practical, non-mystical reality of fifteenth-century farming practices. Unknown author. *The Medieval Plow (Moldboard Plow)*. Drawing, date unknown. Wikimedia Commons. https://commons.wikimedia.org/wiki/File:Plow_medieval.jpg.

Figure 15. Dorio, Lombardy: steep-terraced village on Lake Como. This photograph provides direct geographical corroboration for the decipherment of the toponym "Dorio" on folio 33v. The image of a real-world location with steep, terraced hillsides visually confirms the description of farming on "sloping land" (declivi), anchoring the cipher in verifiable reality. "2022 Dorio" by LauraPiatti. Source: https://commons.wikimedia.org/wiki/File:2022_Dorio.jpg. Licensed under CC BY-SA 4.0 (https://creativecommons.org/licenses/by-sa/4.0/).

Figure 16. Cardoon (*Cynara cardunculus*), thistle-like relative of the artichoke. This botanical illustration identifies the plant discussed in the decipherment of folio 33v. The image confirms that the cardoon, a plant cultivated in Renaissance Italy, is a plausible match for the drawing in the manuscript, linking the decoded text to a real plant and its agricultural history Folio 66r of the Voynich Manuscript (Beinecke MS 408). Early fifteenth century (manuscript.) Beinecke Rare Book & Manuscript Library, Yale University, New Haven, CT, MS 408.. https://collections.library.yale.edu/catalog/2002046?child_oid=1006 139.

Figure 17. Living cardoon showing tall stalks and silvery leaves. This photograph of a living cardoon plant provides a realistic visual reference, allowing a direct comparison with the more stylized drawing in the Voynich Manuscript. It reinforces the identification of the plant on folio 33v as Cynara cardunculus. Mallette, Linnaea. Cardoon Planthttps://commons.wikimedia.org/wiki/File:Cynara_cardunculus _-_Bergianska_tr%C3%A4dg%C3%A5rden_-_Stockholm,_Sweden_-_DSC00304.JPG. CC0 1.0 Universal (CC0 1.0).

Figure 18. Globe artichoke, a cultivated variety of Cynara cardunculus. This image shows a close relative of the cardoon, illustrating the botanical family discussed in Chapter 3. The artichoke's propagation from offshoots provides an important parallel for the decoded phrase "cardoon shoots" (cacti rami), supporting the historical and agronomic plausibility of the text. H. Zell. *Cynara cardunculus* (Globe Artichoke), developing infructescences. Photograph, July 15, 2011. Wikimedia Commons. https://commons.wikimedia.org/wiki/File:Globe_artichoke_Cynara _cardunculus_at_Riverside_Moorings,_Shoreham,_West_Sussex,_En gland.jpg. Creative Commons Attribution-Share Alike 3.0 Unported.

Figure 19. Panoramic view of Amelia (Ameria) in Umbria. This photograph serves as geographical evidence for the decipherment of "Ameria" on the Rosettes foldout. The image of the ancient Italian hill town provides a real-world anchor for the castle depicted in the manuscript, strengthening the claim that the foldout is a conceptual map tied to a specific location. Arcanma. Amelia panorama. Photograph, October 29, 2016. Wikimedia Commons. https://commons.wikimedia.org/wiki/File:Amelia_panorama.jpg. Creative Commons Attribution-Share Alike 4.0 International.

Figure 20. This conceptual image connects the deciphered phrase "*O Ameria rosari*" ("O Ameria of the rose garden") to the dual meaning of rosarium. It represents both a literal rose garden, important in pharmacology, and a metaphorical collection of secrets, linking the location to the book's theme of healing knowledge. Rosarium in Ameria—'*O Ameria rosari*" motif in the foldout. Voynich Manuscript (MS 408), f. 86r (detail). Early fifteenth century. Ink on vellum. Beinecke Rare Book & Manuscript Library, Yale University, New Haven, CT. https://collections.library.yale.edu/catalog/2002046?child_oid=1006 231. Public Domain.

Figure 21. Panoramic view of Kos (Cos) island in the Aegean Sea. This image shows the origin of the famed "Coan wine" mentioned in the central instruction of the Rosettes foldout. The reference to this specific, historically significant medicinal wine, known since antiquity, links the manuscript's pharmacology to classical sources like Pliny the Elder. File:Kos by Sentinel-2 Cloudless.jpg—Wikimedia Commons. By EOX IT Services GmbH is licensed under a Creative Commons Attribution 4.0 International License.

Figure 22. A wine shop attached to the House of Neptune and Amphitrite. This is one of the best-preserved shops in Herculaneum. It has many amphorae and carbonized wood from what were once balustrades and partitions. These ancient wine jars provide a material analog for the cadus (jar) mentioned in the Coan wine cipher. This image helps visualize the practical instruction to add a jar of wine to a mixing vat, grounding the deciphered text in the material culture of classical and Renaissance winemaking and pharmacy. Wikimedia Commons. https://commons.wikimedia.org/wiki/File:Herculaneum_%E2%80 %94_House_of_Neptune_and_Amphitrite_(14732589599).jpg. This image was originally posted to Flickr by Amphipolis at https://flickr.com/photos/35906417@N07/14732589599. It was reviewed on 1 November 2016 by FlickreviewR and was confirmed to be licensed under the terms of the cc-by-sa-2.0.

Figure 23. Iris graminea—source of the "iris-root" plaster. This botanical image identifies the key ingredient in the surgical plaster διὰ χυλῶν (diachýlōn) described on folio 66r. Iris, or orris root, was a well-documented anti-inflammatory in medieval pharmacopoeia, and this identification provides direct pharmacological corroboration for the deciphered text. *Iridaceae - Iris graminea.JPG* by Hectonichus, used under the Creative Commons Attribution-Share Alike 3.0 Unported license. Source: https://commons.wikimedia.org/wiki/File:Iridaceae_- _Iris_graminea.JPG License: https://creativecommons.org/licenses/ by/sa/3.0/deed.en

Figure 24. (folio 66r, zoom in view of patient) Applying a διὰ χυλῶν (diachýlōn) plaster to a patient—medieval/earlymodern practice. Context: Diachylon was a lead-based plaster compounded with oils and herbs for wounds. In plain terms, a sticky medicinal bandage you'd press on after cutting and cauterizing. https://collections.library.yale.edu/catalog/2002046?child_oid=1006 192. https://collections.library.yale.edu/catalog/2002046?child_oid=1006 088.

Figure 25. *Roman Surgical Instruments-Forceps etc.* Found at Pompeii. National Museum Naples. Wellcome Images: Keywords: surgical instruments- rome; history of surgical instruments. This file comes from the Wellcome Collection, a website operated by Wellcome Trust, a global charitable foundation based in the United Kingdom. This file comes from the Wellcome Collection, a website operated by Wellcome Trust, a global charitable foundation based in the United Kingdom. https://commons.wikimedia.org/wiki/File:Roman_surgical_instrum ents-_Forceps_etc._Wellcome_M0004995.jpg. Wellcome Collection gallery (2018-04-02): Roman surgical instruments from Pompeii (M0004995). Credit: Wellcome Collection. Licensed under Attribution 4.0 International (CC BY 4.0).https://wellcomecollection.org/works/yct99mnk CC-BY-4.0.

Figure 26. *Roman Surgical Instruments.* National Archaeological Museum of Naples: 4: Specillum (Probe/Sound). Pompeii. 1st century AD. Bronze. 5: Bisturí (Scalpel). Pompeii. 1st century AD. Bronze. 6: Instrumento ortopédico (Orthopedic instrument). Pompeii. 1st century AD. Bronze. 7: Catéter (Catheter). Pompeii. 1st century AD. Bronze. 8: Retractor (Retractor). Pompeii. 1st century AD. Bronze. 9: Pinzas (Forceps/Pincers). Pompeii. 1st century AD. Bronze.November 18, 2022. Wikimedia Commons. Instrumentos quirúrgicos romanos. Museo Arqueológico Nacional de Nápoles. Credit: Jerónimo Roure Pérez (Dorieo) via Wikimedia Commons. Licensed under Attribution-ShareAlike 4.0 International (CC BY-SA 4.0). https://commons.wikimedia.org/wiki/File:Instrumentos_quir%C3% BArgicos_romanos._Museo_Arqueol%C3%B3gico_Nacional_de_N %C3%A1poles.jpg .

Figure 27. Folio 66r of the Voynich Manuscript (Beinecke MS 408). Early fifteenth century (manuscript.) Beinecke Rare Book &

Manuscript Library, Yale University, New Haven, CT, MS 408. https://collections.library.yale.edu/catalog/2002046?child_oid=1006 192.

Figure 28. Teasel (*Dipsacus sylvestris*). This image identifies one of the two key ingredients in the hemorrhoid remedy deciphered from folio 6v. The historical use of teasel root for treating anal fissures and fistulae, documented by classical authorities like Dioscorides, provides strong pharmacological evidence for the validity of the decipherment. Wisconsin Department of Natural Resources. Common Teasel (Dipsacus fullonum). Photograph. https://commons.wikimedia.org/wiki/File:Dipsacus_fullonum_2011 0625_105347_Berango_43p345889N_2p981917W_r.jpg. Photo by Jon Peli Oleaga Olabarria. This file is licensed under the Creative Commons Attribution-Share Alike 3.0 Unported license.

Figure 29. Castor oil plant (*Ricinus communis*). This image identifies the second ingredient in the folio 6v remedy. Castor oil (oleum cici) was a known topical anti-inflammatory in classical and medieval medicine. Its combination with teasel for a rectal ailment aligns perfectly with historical sources, reinforcing the authenticity of the decoded recipe. Folio 6v of the Voynich Manuscript (Beinecke MS 408). Early fifteenth century (manuscript.) Beinecke Rare Book & Manuscript Library, Yale University, New Haven, CT, MS 408. https://collections.library.yale.edu/catalog/2002046?child_oid=1006 088.

Figure 30. *Pliny the Elder* (AD 23/24–79). This portrait represents one of the foundational classical authorities for the medical and botanical knowledge presented in the book. Pliny's *Naturalis Historia* was a key source for any educated fifteenth-century practitioner, and the deciphered remedies in Codex Obscura frequently align with the uses he documented. https://commons.wikimedia.org/wiki/File:Pliny_the_Elder.png. Public Domain.

Figure 31. Groundsel (*Senecio vulgaris*). This image identifies the plant on folio 6r by its attested medieval Latin name, avia. The plant was known since antiquity for its potent medicinal properties, and its identification is the first step in decoding the folio's alchemical procedure. Folio 6r of the Voynich Manuscript (Beinecke MS 408). Early fifteenth century (manuscript.) Beinecke Rare Book & Manuscript Library, Yale University, New Haven, CT, MS 408.. https://collections.library.yale.edu/catalog/2002046?child_oid=1006 086.

Figure 32. Closeup of groundsel showing nectar glands of an aphid (the "dew"). This image illustrates the ecological interaction central to the alchemical operation on folio 6r. The droplet of honeydew secreted by aphids is interpreted as the "singular sap" (*oenus lac*) or quintessence that the practitioner seeks to harvest, a moment of acute empirical observation captured in the manuscript's drawing. Photo by Sten Porse. https://commons.wikimedia.org/wiki/File:Aphid-shedding-honeydew.jpg. This file is licensed under the Creative Commons Attribution-Share Alike 3.0 Unported, 2.5 Generic, 2.0 Generic and 1.0 Generic license.

Figure 33. Woodcut from *Herbarius—Gart der Gesundheit* (*Hortus sanitatis*), hand-colored, fifteenth/sixteenth century. This comparative illustration from a fifteenth-century German herbal contextualizes the Voynich manuscript's botanical drawings. It shows the contemporary approach to botanical illustration, blending observation with stylization, demonstrating that the Voynich herbal folios were part of a broader tradition of creating illustrated compendia of plant knowledge. Schönsperger, Hans, the Elder (publisher). Plate from *Herbarius—Gart der Gesundheit—Hortus sanitatis*. Augsburg, 1485. Hand-colored woodcut. The Metropolitan Museum of Art, New York. https://www.metmuseum.org/art/collection/search/343821. CC0 1.0 Universal (CC0 1.0) Public Domain Dedication.

Figure 34. The Urbino studiolo—intarsia "cabinet of curiosities" of Duke Federico da Montefeltro. This image of the Duke of Urbino's private study, with its intricate wood-inlay panels depicting scientific instruments and books, embodies the Renaissance fusion of art, science, and power. It represents the kind of secretive, scholarly court

environment that would have valued and potentially produced a ciphered handbook like the Voynich Manuscript. Unknown author. Fifteenth-century intarsia paneling of the Palazzo Ducale, Urbino studiolo. Photograph. Wikimedia Commons. https://commons.wikimedia.org/wiki/File:Studiolo_from_the_Duca l_Palace_in_Gubbio_MET_DT2954.jpg.
Rogers Fund, 1939.

Figure 35. *Pedro Berruguete: Federico da Montefeltro and His Son Guidobaldo.* This portrait shows Duke Federico da Montefeltro, a great condottiero and patron of the arts, in his study, clad in armor but reading a book. The image symbolizes the ideal of the Renaissance ruler who combined military prowess with humanist learning, the very type of patron for whom a work like the Voynich Manuscript would have been created. Berruguete, Pedro (attrib.). *Federico da Montefeltro and His Son Guidobaldo.* Oil on panel, c. 1475. Galleria Nazionale delle Marche, Urbino. Wikimedia Commons. https://commons.wikimedia.org/wiki/File:Pedro_berruguete_federi co_da_montefeltro_e_figlio.jpg.

Figure 36. Bust of Cicco Simonetta (1410–1480), cipher secretary to the Sforza court. This image gives a face to the sophisticated cryptographic world of fifteenth-century Italy. As a key figure in the Sforza court's intelligence operations, Simonetta represents the high-stakes environment of statecraft and secrecy from which the advanced cryptographic techniques seen in the Voynich Manuscript likely emerged. Unknown author. Bust of Cicco Simonetta. Terracotta, fifteenth century. Sforza Castle Civic Museums, Milan. Photograph by G.dallorto. Wikimedia Commons. https://commons.wikimedia.org/wiki/File:Cicco_Simonetta_Como.j pg.

Figure 37. Boötes from Johann Bayer's *Uranometria* (1602). This historical star chart illustrates the constellation Boötes, which is explicitly named in the deciphered text of folio 68r. Its inclusion serves as an astronomical anchor, confirming that the manuscript's celestial diagrams are not abstract fantasies but are grounded in the observable northern sky as cataloged by astronomers like Ptolemy and Bayer.

Bayer, Johann. Boötes. Engraving by Alexander Mair from *Uranometria*, 1602. The Huntington Library, Art Museum, and Botanical   Gardens. https://commons.wikimedia.org/wiki/File:Bootes_-_Johann_Bayer.jpg.

Figure 38. Ursa Minor and Polaris, the pole star about which the heavens appear to turn. This image of the "Little Dipper" and the North Star provides a modern visual reference for the celestial region depicted on folio 68r. The constellation's eternal rotation around the fixed pole star is the physical basis for the book's interpretation of the folio as a diagram of cosmic sovereignty, ruled by a celestial "King." https://commons.wikimedia.org/wiki/File:Ursa_Major_-_Ursa_Minor_-_Polaris.jpg. This file is licensed under the Creative Commons Attribution-Share Alike 3.0 Unported license. Author: Bonc.

Figure 39. Ptolemaic geocentric system: nested crystalline spheres. This diagram illustrates the Earth-centered model of the universe that was the standard scientific framework in the fifteenth century. The concepts of a fixed celestial pole (cardo) and rotating celestial spheres are foundational to this model and are shown to be central to the Voynich manuscript's cosmology. The Ptolemaic geocentric planetary model.   Diagram,   Wikimedia   Commons. https://commons.wikimedia.org/wiki/File:Cellarius_ptolemaic_system.jpg.

Figure 40. Fortune's Wheel from a French Boethius manuscript. This manuscript illumination depicts the famous medieval allegory of the Wheel of Fortune. It provides the philosophical context for the manuscript's cosmology, illustrating the Boethian idea that the chaotic turnings of earthly fate are contrasted with the serene, predictable order of the heavens. Coëtivy Master (Henri de Vulcop?, attr.). *Philosophy Consoling Boethius and Fortune Turning the Wheel.* Illuminated manuscript leaf, c. 1460–70. J. Paul Getty Museum (MS 42), Los Angeles.   Wikimedia   Commons. https://commons.wikimedia.org/wiki/File:Boethius,_Consolatio_philosophiae_(French).jpg.

Figure 41. Boethius teaching— illuminated initial. This illumination, showing the philosopher Boethius teaching his students, represents the profound influence of his work, *The Consolation of Philosophy*, on medieval and Renaissance thought. It reinforces the claim that the Voynich author was participating in a living intellectual tradition that saw the cosmos through a Boethian lens. Unknown author. Initial depicting Boethius teaching his students. Manuscript illumination from *Consolation of Philosophy*, Italy, 1385. Wikimedia Commons. illuminated initial. This illumination, showing the philosopher Boethius teaching his students, represents the profound influence of his work, The Consolation of Philosophy, on medieval and Renaissance thought. It reinforces the claim that the Voynich author was participating in a living intellectual tradition that saw the cosmos through a Boethian lens. Unknown author. Initial depicting Boethius teaching his students. Manuscript illumination from Consolation of Philosophy, Italy, 1385. Wikimedia Commons. https://commons.wikimedia.org/wiki File:Boethius_initial_consolation_philosophy.jpg. Public Domain.

Figure 42. Rota Caeli—medieval diagram of the "wheel of the heavens." This type of medieval diagram, which depicts the concentric motions of the celestial spheres, serves as a conceptual parallel to the astronomical charts in the Voynich Manuscript. It illustrates the idea of the heavens as a divine clock, used for determining auspicious timing for earthly actions like medicine and alchemy. Folio 68r of the Voynich Manuscript (Beinecke MS 408). Early fifteenth century (manuscript.) Beinecke Rare Book & Manuscript Library, Yale University, New Haven, CT, MS 408. https://collections.library.yale.edu/catalog/2002046?child_oid=1006 196.

Figure 43. Title page of *Polygraphiae* (1518), by Johannes Trithemius. This image shows the title page of the first printed book on cryptography. Its inclusion demonstrates that the secret arts of ciphering, which the Voynich author practiced, were beginning to be systematized and published, marking the transition of cryptography from a guarded secret to a teachable science. Trithemius, Johannes. *Polygraphiae by Johannes Trithemius, 1518, stated to be the first published book on cryptology - National Cryptologic Museum - DSC07742.JPG.* Photograph by Daderot. Sourced from Wikimedia Commons,. The work has been dedicated to the public domain via Creative Commons CC0 1.0 Universal Public Domain Dedication (http://creativecommons.org/publicdomain/zero/1.0/deed.en).

Figure 44. Urbino studiolo. This alternate view of the Duke of Urbino's study further illustrates the intellectual environment of a fifteenth-century court. The combination of scholarly pursuits and symbols of power reflects the world in which a secret, practical handbook like the Voynich Manuscript would have been a prized possession. Studiolo from the Ducal Palace in Gubbio. Walnut, beech, rosewood, oak, and fruitwoods, c. 1478–82. The Metropolitan Museum of Art, New York. https://commons.wikimedia.org/wiki/File:
Studiolo_from_the_Ducal_Palace_in_Gubbio_MET_DT213911.jpg. This file is made available under the Creative Commons CC0 1.0 Universal Public Domain Dedication.

Figure 45. Claudius Ptolemy (c. 100–c. 170 AD). This portrait represents the ancient authority whose geocentric model of the cosmos dominated scientific thought for over 1,400 years. The deciphered cosmology of the Voynich Manuscript is shown to be firmly rooted in Ptolemy's system, demonstrating the author's engagement with the foundational scientific texts of the era. Painting by Justus van Gent. *Claudius Ptolemy*. Oil painting on canvas. Wikimedia Commons.
https://commons.wikimedia.org/wiki/File:Plate_XLVIII_-
DPLA-_3315b8372a64fdadd7616cd0c1f48b94.jpg. The author died in 1480, so this work is in the public domain in the United States.

Figure 46. Historic botanical plate (Plate XLVIII): pharmacognosy context for herbal folios. This example of a traditional botanical plate provides a comparative context for the Voynich's herbal section. It highlights the conventional format of pairing a plant illustration with a textual description of its properties, a format that the Voynich Manuscript follows, albeit with an unreadable script and often unidentifiable plants. Blackwell, Elizabeth. Plate 48 from *A Curious*

Herbal. 1737. Wikimedia Commons. https://commons.wikimedia.org/wiki/File:Plate_XLVIII_-_DPLA_-_3315b8372a64fdadd7616cd0c1f48b94.jpg. Public Domain.

Figure 47. Francesco Sforza (1401–1466). This portrait of the Duke of Milan places the manuscript within the political and cultural orbit of one of fifteenth-century Italy's most powerful courts. The Sforza court was a known center for cryptographic innovation, providing a plausible environment for the development and use of the manuscript's advanced cipher. By Bembo, Bonifazio? *Portrait of Francesco Sforza.* Miniature in the manuscript Milan, *Biblioteca Trivulziana*, 786, fol. 1 (inserted folio). Wikimedia Commons. https://commons.wikimedia.org/wiki/File:Francesco_Sforza,_Trivul ziana_786.jpg. Public Domain.

Figure 48. William F. Friedman (1891–1969). This photograph of the renowned twentieth-century cryptanalyst represents the formidable challenge the Voynich Manuscript has posed to modern codebreakers. Friedman's conclusion that the script was likely an artificial language is a major counter-theory that the book directly addresses and refutes. Unknown author. William F. Friedman. Photograph, date unknown. National Security Agency. Wikimedia Commons. File:William-Friedman.jpg—Wikimedia Commons. Public Domain (PD-USGov-NSA).

Figure 49. Folio 99v of the Voynich Manuscript (Beinecke MS 408). Early fifteenth century (manuscript.) Beinecke Rare Book & Manuscript Library, Yale University, New Haven, CT, MS 408. Apothecary jars. This image of Renaissance-era pharmacy jars illustrates the material culture of the world from which the Voynich Manuscript's recipes and remedies emerged. These vessels would have held the very tinctures, plasters, and herbal compounds whose preparation is described in the deciphered text https://collections.library.yale.edu/catalog/2002046?child_oid=1006 247.

CONSOLIDATED BIBLIOGRAPHY

Alberti, Leon Battista. "De componendis cifris." In The Mathematical Works of Leon Battista Alberti, edited and translated by Kim Williams, Lionel March, and Stephen R. Wassell, 169–181. Basel: Birkhäuser, 2010.

Allen, Richard Hinckley. *Star Names: Their Lore and Meaning.* New York: G. E. Stechert, 1899. Republication, New York: Dover, 1963.

Avicenna (Ibn Sina). *The Canon of Medicine of Avicenna.* Translated by O. Cameron Gruner. London: Luzac & Co., 1930. Reprint, New York: AMS Press, 1973

Barabe, Joseph G. "Material Analysis of the Voynich Manuscript." Report, McCrone Associates, Inc., Westmont, IL, April 22, 2009.

Boethius, Anicius Manlius Severinus. *The Consolation of Philosophy.* Translated by Richard H. Green. Indianapolis: Bobbs-Merrill, 1962.

Buonafalce, Augusto. "Cicco Simonetta's Cipher-Breaking Rules." *Cryptologia* 32, no. 1 (2008): 62-70.

Cato the Elder. *On Agriculture.* In *Marcus Porcius Cato on Agriculture and Marcus Terentius Varro on Agriculture.* Translated by W. D. Hooper, revised by H. B. Ash. Loeb Classical Library 283. Cambridge, MA: Harvard University Press, 1934.

Crescenzi, Pietro de'. *Ruralia Commoda.* Augsburg: Johann Schüssler, 1471.

Dioscorides, Pedanius. *De Materia Medica.* Translated by Lily Y. Beck. Hildesheim: Olms-Weidmann, 2005.

Getz, Faye. *Healing and Society in Medieval England.* Madison: University of Wisconsin Press, 1991.

Green, Monica H. "The Doctor's Cipher: Literacy, Secrecy, and Authority in Medieval Medicine." *Speculum* 89, no. 2 (2014): 398-435.

Hale, J. R. Renaissance Fortification: Art or Engineering? London: Thames and Hudson, 1977.

Hauer, Bradley, and Grzegorz Kondrak. "Decoding Anagrammed Texts Written in an Unknown Language and Script." *Transactions of the Association for Computational Linguistics* 4 (2016): 75-86.

Hodgins, Greg. "Radiocarbon Dating of the Voynich Manuscript." Presentation, University of Arizona, Tucson, AZ, February 10, 2011.

Hunt, Arnold. "Voynich the Buyer." In *The Voynich Manuscript*, edited by Raymond Clemens, 11–21. New Haven: Yale University Press, 2016.

Kahn, David. The Codebreakers: The Comprehensive History of Secret Communication from Ancient Times to the Internet. 2nd ed. New York: Scribner, 1996.

Landini, Gabriel. "Zipf's Law and the Voynich Manuscript." *Cryptologia* 25, no. 4 (2001): 277-288.

Larner, John. Italy in the Age of Dante and Petrarch, 1216-1380. London: Longman, 1980.

Meister, Aloys. Die Anfänge der modernen diplomatischen Geheimschrift. Paderborn: F. Schöningh, 1902.

Nauert, Jr., Charles G. *Humanism and the Culture of Renaissance Europe.* 2nd ed. Cambridge: Cambridge University Press, 2006.

Park, Katharine. Secrets of Women: Gender, Generation, and the Origins of Human Dissection. New York: Zone Books, 2006.

Pelling, Nick. "Fifteenth Century Cryptography." Cipher Mysteries (blog), July 6, 2016.

Pliny the Elder. *Natural History*. Translated by H. Rackham. 10 vols. Loeb Classical Library. Cambridge, MA: Harvard University Press, 1938-1962.

Principe, Lawrence M. *The Secrets of Alchemy*. Chicago: University of Chicago Press, 2013.

Ptolemy. *Ptolemy's Almagest*. Translated by G.J. Toomer. Princeton: Princeton University Press, 1998.

Riddle, John M. Goddesses, Elixirs, and Witches: Potions and Spells from Garden to Glass. New York: Palgrave Macmillan, 2024.

Rugg, Gordon. "An Elegant Hoax? A Possible Solution to the Voynich Manuscript." *Cryptologia* 28, no. 1 (2004): 31-46.

Siraisi, Nancy G. Medieval & Early Renaissance Medicine: An Introduction to Knowledge and Practice. Chicago: University of Chicago Press, 1990.

Smith, William, ed. *A Dictionary of Greek and Roman Antiquities*. London: John Murray, 1875.

Trithemius, Johannes. *Polygraphiae Libri Sex*. Oppenheim: Johann Haselberg, 1518.

Tucker, Arthur O., and Jules Janick. *Unraveling the Voynich Codex*. Cham: Springer, 2018.

University of Arizona. "Radiocarbon Dating of the Voynich Manuscript." Press Conference, February 2011.

Vespasiano da Bisticci. *The Vespasiano Memoirs: Lives of Illustrious Men of the XVth Century*. Translated by William George and Emily Waters. London: Routledge & Kegan Paul, 1926.

Zandbergen, René. "Earliest Owners." In *The Voynich Manuscript*, edited by Raymond Clemens, 1–10. New Haven: Yale University Press, 2016.

www.ingramcontent.com/pod-product-compliance
Lightning Source LLC
Chambersburg PA
CBHW051616120626
46551CB00014B/1825